A Guide Through

C.S.LEWIS' SpaceTrilogy

D1566078

A Guide Through

C.S.LEWIS'
Space Trilogy

By Martha C. Sammons

Cornerstone Books • Westchester, Illinois

To Marty and Marci

Grateful acknowledgement is made for permission to quote from *Out of the Silent Planet* by C.S. Lewis, published in the U.S. by Macmillan Publishing Co., Inc., 1945; and from *Perelandra* by C. S. Lewis, copyright 1944 by C. S. Lewis renewed 1972 by Alfred Cecil Harwood and Arthur O. Barfield; and from *That Hideous Strength* by C.S. Lewis copyright 1945, 1946 by C.S. Lewis renewed 1973, 1974 by Alfred Cecil Harwood and Arthur O. Barfield. All reprinted with permission of Macmillan Publishing Co., Inc.

Illustrations by Ellie Arnot.

First printing, 1980

Printed in the United States of America

Library of Congress Catalog Card Number 80-68329
ISBN 0-89107-185-7

In the beginning Maleldil created the heavens and the earth,
the Great Dance.
Wove the pattern,
Sang into being
Arbol and Sulva,
Lurga and Glund,
Viritrilbia and Earth,
Malacandra and Perelandra,
Lady and King,
eldil and hross,
sorn and pfifltrigg,
talking beast, singing beast,
tree and leaf,
fruit and seed,
dust and grain.

The heel was bitten.

And the Music no longer sung,
The Voice in the Garden no longer heard,
The Light made shadow,
The Full made empty,
The "Shining One" cast down.
What was One, separate,
What was Straight, bent,
The Great War begun.

The silence shall cease.
The Bent shall be broken.
For His Name also is Ransom.

The Crooked met the Straight,
And what was wounded shall become Whole.
The lame shall leap for Joy.

Martha C. Sammons

CONTENTS

INTRODUCTION

C. S. Lewis's science fiction or "Ransom" trilogy—*Out of the Silent Planet, Perelandra,* and *That Hideous Strength*—has become perhaps one of his most widely known works, as well as a milestone in science fiction or space fantasy writing. Since publication, over 2,185,000 copies of the trilogy have been sold, and they can be found on the shelves of almost any bookstore. They are unique not only because Lewis is known mainly as a writer of religious books, literary criticism, and his seven children's stories *(The Chronicles of Narnia),* but because they bring religious themes to science fiction. Giving the biblical story of man's fall and its blot on the glory of the universe a new form, the trilogy jolts us into a different way of seeing history and the future of the cosmos.

Actually, the term *science fiction* is not totally descriptive of the *kind* of books they are. Let us say Lewis has created his own myth of Deep Heaven that carries us through the tingling and vibrant heavens to Mars, Venus, and back to earth again as the stage of a great battle. This myth is woven from a variety of elements, from medieval views of the universe to Arthurian legend and biblical stories. It examines modern "scientism" and its tampering with Nature, our misconceptions about alien creatures, man and his place in the tapestry of the universe, the nature of evil and its slick, disguising powers, marital problems, and the story of two special and troubled lives, Jane and Mark Studdock. Thus, the books seem to be even more up-to-date than they were in the forties! And the stories and scenes are as diverse as sorns, hrossa, eldila, the Green Lady, a bubbling green Head, and lovable Bultitude, or pink and purple *handramits,* floating islands, or the sprawling mansion of Belbury.

Since the books are based on so many sources and tell Lewis's own elaborate "mythic" version of the Christian story, they might seem a bit confusing on first reading. *Perelandra's* sustained temptation scene may seem a bit long, or *That Hideous Strength* too packed with ideas. Thus, the purpose of this "guide" will be to set forth Lewis's mythology, tell you why and how he came to write his myth, introduce you to the background of his sources—medieval, Arthurian, and biblical—and discuss their many themes. The dictionaries include Lewis's invented languages; the names, places, and allusions in the stories; and their meaning and origin. Those who have read the trilogy only once, or have not been through it in some time, may want to read the Appendix as a review.

In the final chapters of *Out of the Silent Planet,* Lewis and Ransom decide to publish in fictional form what they believe is fact because they want to reach a wider public. If only a handful of people are reached, they say, it will be well worth it. Because earth is in such danger right now, a group of people with a certain set of ideas is vitally needed. Lewis says he hopes at the very least to change the conception of space to that of Heaven for at least 1 percent of his readers. Certainly, one change you might have felt as you put down each book and looked back on Thulcandra was a renewed view of outer space, alien creatures, your neighbor, our imperiled planet, "religion," and even of each moment as special and filled with surprising possibilities.

The dangers Lewis warned were approaching back in

the forties are becoming realities in our world. For the myth of Deep Heaven is a true story—the story of you, your earth past and future, the choices you will make, and what side you will be on in a present and ever worsening battle: "God will invade. . . . When that happens, it is the end of the world . . . when you see the whole natural universe melting away like a dream and something else—something it never entered your head to conceive—comes crashing in; something so beautiful to some of us and so terrible to others that none of us will have any choice left . . . it will be the time when we discover which side we really have chosen."

CHAPTER 1: MAKER OF MYTHS: C. S. LEWIS AND SCIENCE FICTION

All things are by Him and for Him. He utters
Himself also for His own delight and sees
that He is good. He is His own begotten and
what proceeds from Him is Himself. Blessed
be He!

C. S. Lewis, born in Belfast in 1898, was a literature professor at Oxford University and not unlike his hero Ransom. He is known as a writer of religious books (such as *Mere Christianity, The Problem of Pain, The Screwtape Letters,* and *Miracles*) and of literary criticism (such as *The Allegory of Love* and *Preface to Paradise Lost*). His seven children's books, *The Chronicles of Narnia,* are unlike anything else he ever wrote and may very well become classics of children's literature. Why, then, would he write three "planetary" science fiction novels?

Actually, Lewis had always been a science fiction reader. In fact, one of the Boxen stories which he wrote as a child is called "To Mars and Back." In his autobiography, he wrote of his childhood: "The idea of other planets exercised upon me then a peculiar, heady attraction, which was quite different from any other of my literary interests. . . . The interest, when the fit was upon me, was ravenous, like a lust. . . . I may perhaps add that my own planetary romances have been not so much the gratification of that fierce curiosity as its exorcism. The exorcism worked by reconciling it with, or subjecting it to, the other, the more elusive, and genuinely imaginative, impulse."

By the 1930s, so many major changes had taken place in science fiction that Lewis decided it was time to react against them. What had developed was the pulpy "scientification" story begun by writers such as American Hugo Gernsback, who developed the magazine you can still find on newsstands, *Amazing Stories*. Such science fiction dealt with the weird, amazing, romantic, and technological, but its main purpose was to concentrate on science—to disseminate new theories and speculations—rather than plot or character. As might be expected, this trend was accompanied by a plethora of science fiction clubs and fanzines. So, Weston is appropriately described as "a man obsessed with the idea which at this moment was circulating all over our planet in obscure works of 'scientification' in little Interplanetary Societies and Rocketry Clubs, and between covers of monstrous magazines."

Lewis thought too much science and too little fiction was produced by such scientification. In fact, he was totally uninterested in the purely technical side of his own stories. He confessed, for example, that the propelling of his spaceship in *Out of the Silent Planet* by some lesser known properties of solar radiation was "pure mumbo jumbo." But he did try to introduce just enough "fact" to make his story plausible and to encourage his readers to become really involved in the action.

For instance, the only details Lewis includes about the means of space travel are that Weston, Devine, and Ransom journey for twenty-eight days in a spherical metallic spaceship with crystal and wire instruments. Since the center is always down in this sphere, the floor you are standing on feels flat and horizontal, and the wall you lean against feels vertical. In *Perelandra,* Ransom is simply transported in a white coffin moved by the Oyarsa in a sort of state of suspended animation.

To make *Out of the Silent Planet* more "believable," Lewis intrudes as narrator in the final chapter to tell how the story was *really* written. He claims that he knew Ransom for several years, though they had not met, and corresponded with him on literary and philological subjects. When Lewis, quite by coincidence, wrote Ransom a letter asking whether he knew what an "Oyarsa" is, Ransom was naturally triggered into telling his amazing tale. Certain that the world would not believe them, but that the dangers facing earth are gravely cosmic and eternal, they decide they cannot be silent. So Ransom suggests they publish fact in the form of fiction to reach a greater public. It is important that at least some readers become familiar with certain ideas. Ransom tacks on a postscript to their account, providing even more details about Malacandra. He even chastises Lewis for omitting from his fictionalized version the fact that the reason they suffered so from excess light just before their landing on Malacandra is that their shutter jammed. Ransom feels sure readers would notice and wonder about that little detail.

Perelandra is cleverly told within a slightly different framework to add credibility. Lewis tells how with great misgivings he prepared Ransom for a second journey, nailed him into a coffin, and then how Ransom returned over a year later. He then relates the story as Ransom told it to him, but manages to maintain suspense even though we know Ransom made it through safely. *That Hideous Strength,* unlike the first two stories, is related by a more impersonal narrator who simply tells us he was born in Cambridge, was Oxford-bred, and actually visited Bragdon Wood himself. In order to give a wider perspective and objectively tell details about the Studdocks, Lewis focuses much less on Ransom.

Like his friend J. R. R. Tolkien, Lewis firmly believed

that good fantasy writing should never break the spell or bring the reader back to earth with a bump. Instead, it should make the reader *feel* instead of simply telling him, and it should make something "happen" once he has gotten to the other world, such as high, reckless, heroic, romantic wars. At the same time, Lewis was irked by people ("in Interplanetary Societies") who take fantasy as 100 percent real and possible in this world. For this reason, many have argued that Lewis's books are not properly science fiction at all. Science fiction, after all, is usually defined as a projection of what science knows or where theories may lead, whereas Lewis admittedly was uninterested in scientific accuracy. Still, he believed science fiction is important because it can deal with key issues, such as human destiny, far more seriously and effectively than "realistic" fiction can. And certainly his books, whatever "type" they are, fulfill that goal!

Traditional writers of science fiction seem always to show aliens as monsters or ogres and terrestrial invaders as good and ever in the right. A perfect example can be found in *The War of the Worlds* by H. G. Wells, who was a major influence on Lewis's own books: "Those who have never seen a living Martian can scarcely imagine the strange horror of its appearance. The peculiar V-shaped mouth with its pointed upper lips, the absence of brow ridges, the absence of a chin beneath the wedgelike lower lip, the incessant quivering of this mouth, the Gorgon groups of tentacles . . . the extraordinary intensity of the immense eyes—were at once vital, intense, inhuman, crippled and monstrous."

Lewis believed his trilogy began the trend of showing the opposite to be true. How wrong Ransom finds all his expectations about Mars, sorns, and hrossa to be! In fact, the writing of the space trilogy may have begun as a wager with J. R. R. Tolkien, who also believed there was too little of what they liked in stories. So the two decided they would have to write some themselves. Lewis was to write about space and Tolkien about time (no doubt, the vast history of Middle-earth). Lewis felt he was trying to "redeem" the science fiction form for imaginative purposes.

He also classified science fiction into several "types," only one of which he truly enjoyed. First and worst is the type that uses science fiction merely as a backdrop for a love, spy, wreck, or crime story that could just as well have taken place anywhere. The second type is interested in space travel or other undiscovered techniques as real possibilities (e.g., Jules Verne's *20,000 Leagues Under the Sea*, which anticipates our modern submarine).

The third is speculative—for example, what is such and such a planet or experience like? Such a work is H. G. Wells's *The First Men in the Moon* (1901), which Lewis felt was the best of this sort he had read and Wells's best novel. Although he liked the "pure fantasy" of Wells's novels, Lewis did not enjoy the sermonizing and didacticism. But Wells's story, which has much in common with *Out of the Silent Planet*, was inspiration for Lewis's book: "The author would be sorry if any reader supposed he was too stupid to have enjoyed Mr. H. G. Wells's fantasies or too ungrateful to acknowledge his debt to them." Lewis's other "space" story, *The Dark Tower*, which we shall look at later, was perhaps a reply to Wells's *The Time Machine*.

In *The First Men in the Moon*, we have a chance meeting with Cavor, an eccentric scientist like Weston, and a spherical spaceship built to go to the moon. The narrator, like Ransom, believes space will be unfathomably dark and cold, but finds the sensations pleasurable and his vision of the star-dusted sky unforgettable. The travelers must acclimatize to the new environment, become educated to the social structure of the Selenites, and meet the ruler. Wells also concludes with six messages from Cavor similar to Ransom's postscript. In addition, Lewis seems to be answering the question posed in *War of the Worlds* as to whether man will spread from "this little seed bed of the solar system throughout the inanimate vastness of sidereal space" when earth becomes uninhabitable, or whether, instead, other creatures will invade earth.

The fourth type of science fiction, says Lewis, deals with the future—for example, the ultimate destiny of our species. Here Lewis found the greatest influences on his own books: "What immediately spurred me to write was Olaf Stapledon's *Last and First Men* and an essay in J. B. S. Haldane's *Possible Worlds,* both of which seemed to have the desperately immoral outlook which I try to pillory in Weston. I like the whole interplanetary idea as a *mythology* and simply wished to conquer for my own (Christian) point of view what has always hitherto been used by the opposite side."

Lewis admired Stapledon's "invention," but not his philosophy. Stapledon's book *Last and First Men: A Story of the Near and Far Future* (1930) describes, like *That Hideous Strength,* scientists who try to construct a bodiless brain which will dominate them. The book tells the history of man over the next two billion years, including migrations to Venus and Neptune. Stapledon describes the religions characterizing each period and believes man might be "the spark destined to revitalize the cosmos." Lewis, of course, gives this very same philosophy a Christian perspective.

Stapledon also believed in an immaterial Spirit (like Weston's Life-Force) who shaped the universe. Humanity's purpose is to understand and live in harmony with it. Like the philosophy we are warned of in *That Hideous Strength,* Stapledon's view was that the universe is in a state of evolution; so man must improve, not destroy, with his power. This process can only be accomplished by spreading education and by genetic mutation to form a group-mind harnessing the power of many individuals.

Lewis's other influence, J. B. S. Haldane, was a world-famous physiologist, biochemist, geneticist, Marxist, and spokesman of science. Some believe he is represented in the trilogy by Weston. His essays are collected in *Possible Worlds: A Scientist Looks at Science* (1927), but Lewis was particularly interested in the essay, "The Last Judgement." Echoing N.I.C.E., Haldane argues that social problems can only be solved in the long run by application of the scientific method. He is also a defender of vivisection (experimentation with live animals), which of course Lewis deplored. Furthermore, Haldane predicts that if earth ever becomes uninhabitable, man will adapt himself for migration to and colonization of other planets and suns because of "survival instinct." Man must control his own evolution, but only some men will take charge of the destiny of others. Haldane writes: "There is no theoretical limit to man's material progress but the subjection to complete conscious control of every atom and quantum of radiation in the universe. There is, perhaps, no limit at all to his intellectual and spiritual progress." Referring frequently to the shortcomings of Christianity when faced by scientific facts, Haldane believed earth and man cannot possibly be as bad as Christianity makes out. The trilogy, of course, counterattacks all of these ideas.

The last type of science fiction was most desirable to Lewis. In this type—actually what he called the "mythopoeic" novel—the scientific is only a "machine" since the work need only be superficially plausible. Instead, supernatural methods are really the best. This type of novel "adds to life" by giving us sensations we have never had before at a deep level and by enlarging our conceptions of the whole range of possible experiences. The purpose of other planets in science fiction, then, is not for their physical strangeness or spatial distance, but for our need for the idea of "otherness," "wonder," "beauty": "To construct plausible and moving 'other worlds' you must draw on the only real 'other world' we know, that of the spirit."

Lewis preferred a sort of combination of two kinds of fiction as his "ideal"—that of Novalis, George MacDonald, and James Stephens and that of Wells and Verne. Such a story would contain not only space travel, but "gods, ghosts, ghouls, demons, fairies, monsters, etc." Examples of books he thought successful are parts of the *Odyssey* and *Faerie Queene*, Morris's *Earthly Paradise*, MacDonald's books, and Tolkien's *Lord of the Rings*. Lewis himself said that writers such as James Stephens, G. K. Chesterton, William Morris, and George MacDonald influenced his trilogy. The "real father" of his planet books, however, was David Lindsay's *Voyage to Arcturus*. Lindsay gave him the idea that scientification could be combined with the supernatural: "His Tormance is a region of the spirit. He is the first writer to discover what 'other planets' are really good for in fiction." Other influences were medieval astrology, the art of Arthur Rackham, and his whole lifelong love of Norse and Old Icelandic legend. Finally, Lewis said the operatic ending of *Perelandra* was from Wagner's *Ring of the Niebelungen.*

A further impetus for the trilogy was simply Lewis's fear of the real dangers of "Westonism." He wanted to refute the idea he had heard from his students and others that interplanetary colonization is acceptable and necessary for the human race. In fact, one person Lewis talked to told him he pinned all his hopes for any significance in the universe on the chance that the human race, by adapting itself, can jump to other planets, stars, and nebulae forever and subject matter to mind. "I begin to be afraid that the villains will really contaminate the moon," wrote Lewis.

In his "Reply to Professor Haldane," Lewis makes it clear that *Out of the Silent Planet* is thus an attack, not on science, but "scientism"—a certain outlook on the world connected with the popularization of the sciences—which says the species must be perpetuated, even at the loss of pity, happiness, and freedom. Although the book has no factual basis, Lewis called it a critique of our own age, as any Christian work is. At the end of *Out of the Silent Planet,* Lewis tells us he only fictionalized Ransom's factual story in order to reach a greater public and because he felt a body of people familiar with certain ideas was needed.

Out of the Silent Planet was completed by September 1937. After rejections by both J. M. Dent and Allen and Unwin publishers, it was accepted by The Bodley Head and published in the autumn of 1938. Afterwards, Lewis said he got several letters asking if the book was true, so he assumed people just don't understand what "fiction" is. Professor Clyde Kilby, for example, received a letter addressed to Lewis after Lewis's death from a thirteen-year-old girl who wanted Ransom's real name, address, and more information from him about Mars.

She said she thoroughly believed he went to Mars and wanted to compliment him on his writing style!

Lewis probably had an idea of writing a sequel long before *Out of the Silent Planet* was published, but no one is sure what he intended. The end of the novel leaves the way open for a sequel by suggesting that eternal cosmic forces behind Weston will play an important role in the next centuries and will be dangerous if not stopped. Lewis said that the letter at the end of the book, which is also pure fiction, was a way to prepare for a sequel because it ends: "if there is to be any more space-travelling, it will have to be time-travelling as well. . . !"

Lewis wrote only part of a possible sequel. It is called *The Dark Tower* and has been published in *The Dark Tower and Other Stories* by Harcourt, Brace, Jovanovich. This fragment was probably written in 1938 or 1939 and is about time-travel, beginning with a line that links well with the conclusion of *Out of the Silent Planet:* " 'Of course,' said Orfieu, 'the sort of time-travelling you read about in books—time-travelling in the body—is absolutely impossible.' " Ransom appears in the story, described as "the hero, or victim, of one of the strangest adventures that had ever befallen a mortal man."

The fragment is curiously unlike Lewis's other novels with the noticeable absence of any religious ideas. And it is uncertain how he would have gone about developing the strange story to make it technically plausible. But it begins with a scientist named Orfieu discussing the possibilities of time-travel. He shows his assistant Scudamour, MacPhee (who, of course, appears in *That Hideous Strength*), Ransom, and Lewis his invention—a "chronoscope" which can view a time from either past or future. In it they see a Dark Tower (a copy of their new Cambridge library apparently built by a future generation) which exists in a parallel time and universe.

In the tower crouches a man with a poisonous sting on his forehead, and nearby is an idol composed of many human bodies sharing one head (possibly the seed of the "Head" idea in *That Hideous Strength*). The stinging man injects a poison into people's spines, dehumanizing them into automatons which behave as if of one communal mind. Scudamour has a "double" in that world who grows a sting and replaces the stinging man. As he is just about to sting his fianceé, Camilla (the "double" of Scudamour's fianceé and possible namesake of Camilla Denniston), Scudamour suddenly dives at the chronoscope. He exchanges minds with his double, while the latter runs off to hide. Since Orfieu's chronoscope has been ruined, the group is faced with having to build another one and with figuring out how to reexchange the doubles. Just as we see Scudamour doing research on time in the library, the fragment ends. Lewis apparently abandoned the whole idea by the end of 1939.

Perelandra began after Lewis completed his book *Preface to Paradise Lost* in the spring of 1941. Again, it was probably not intended as part of a "trilogy" since a trilogy had apparently never been planned. But *Perelandra* arose partly as a result of *Preface to Paradise Lost* when Lewis started thinking about the purpose of the forbidden fruit in the Garden of Eden and realized it was to instill obedience. He also became interested in the nature of an unfallen Adam and Eve.

Actually, Lewis explained that *all* his stories, including *The Chronicles of Narnia* and the three science fiction books, began by seeing mental pictures. Then he had to invent reasons why a character should be in these places and find a proper form (novel, poem, story) for this picture. *Perelandra* grew out of recurring mental pictures of floating islands. He most likely got this image from Stapledon's *Last and First Men* which says: "In the early days of Venus men had gathered foodstuffs from the great floating islands of vegetable matter." Next, said Lewis, he built up a world in which floating islands could exist. Then the story about an averted fall developed. Contrary to what many people think, however, the book did *not* begin with a didactic Christian purpose, moral, or message because Lewis felt the story itself should force its moral on you. In the Preface to *Perelandra*, Lewis is careful to point out that the book is not an allegory—a composition in which immaterial realities or abstract concepts are "represented" by objects, characters, and events (e.g., the Green Lady does not "stand for" Eve). Instead, Lewis saw the book as a "supposition": *suppose* men went to another planet and found unfallen races; "suppose, even now, in some other planet there were a first couple undergoing the same that Adam and Eve underwent here, but successfully." One of Lewis's main goals in writing, in fact, was to give the Christian story fresh excitement by retelling it as a new myth.

By November 9, 1941, he was through the first conversation with the Green Lady and finished the entire book by May 11, 1942. The novel was published in 1943, then reissued under the title *A Voyage to Venus* (Pan Books).* As with *Out of the Silent Planet*, readers found *Perelandra* so convincing that they wrote to Lewis asking for Ransom's address and wanting to compliment him on his heroism, the "good run for his money" that he gave the Devil, and for the realism of his style. But Lewis still felt that most serious reviewers of the book found it unfavorable or were noncommittal about it. While Lewis himself thought *Till We Have Faces* his masterpiece, he liked *Perelandra* the best of all his novels—worth twenty *Screwtapes*—perhaps because he enjoyed its imaginative world so much. He reportedly often said the word "Perelandra" with a longing and passion in his voice as he gazed up at Venus sparkling in the sky. Yet he felt it was a book that was almost impossible to write. The Green Lady, after all, had to not only portray perfect goodness, but had to be both a pagan goddess and a virgin! But he thought it was worth trying, even if he could only partially succeed.

*Shortly before Lewis's death, David Marsh and Donald Swann composed an opera from *Perelandra*. They went over it with Lewis, who supposedly liked the music so well it brought tears to his eyes. It was performed in Oxford, London, and Cambridge several months after his death, as well as in New York City and jointly by Bryn Mawr and Haverford Colleges. Although the score has not been published, it can be borrowed from Galaxy Music Publishers. There is also a tape recording at the Wade Collection at Wheaton College. The substance of the score involves Ransom's attempts to persuade the Green Lady to remain obedient to God and his inner struggle in coping with the Un-man.

In 1943, Lewis delivered his lectures on "The Abolition of Man" at the University of Durham and had also fallen
under the influence of Charles Williams. Both served as major
influences on *That Hideous Strength*. This book was finished
by December 20, 1943, and was published in July 1945, thereby completing the "trilogy," although Lewis says *That
Hideous Strength* can be read on its own. The book sold well,
but Lewis still thought the reviewers and critics hated it,
predominantly because they saw N.I.C.E. as a fantastic
absurdity. In response to a question about making a film version of the book, Lewis joked that this would be difficult because of the rarity of tame angels and bears in England!

One of the main difficulties with the book has always
been the debate about what kind of a novel it actually is. Lewis
calls it a "fairy-tale" for grown-ups because in the fairy-tale
tradition he uses humdrum scenes and persons. But, he adds,
most readers today don't notice the fairy-tale method because
cottages, castles, wood-cutters, and petty kings have become
things of the past. When asked if it is perhaps an epic, Lewis
replied that the book is rather a "romance" because he felt it
does not have enough roots in legend and tradition.

At any rate, the book is a complex mixture of elements, ranging from Arthurian legend and magic and derived
mainly from Charles Williams, the Grail legend, Swiftian satire
of man, Owen Barfield's views of language and man's relation
to the universe, the Tower of Babel and other biblical stories,
and, of course, an entire range of ideas which Lewis is attacking.

Lewis says his book is a " 'tall story' about devilry"
which we will discuss in more detail in Chapter 5, and his
conversations with scientific colleagues. But many people
seem to think of the book as a *1984* or *Brave New World* type
of attack on science. In *Of Other Worlds*, however, Lewis
says scientists were not the target, but rather several other
modern trends: "officials"; use of power by a small group of
people; inner rings (which he saw as the chief theme); exalta-

tion of the "collective," along with growing indifference to individuals themselves; the "Party" which obeys an impersonal force and believes in inevitable progress, which it sees as one's supreme duty to forward even if moral laws are broken; use of scientific planning as a guise for misuse of power; philosophical ideas, such as those of Wither; and modern education, which Lewis felt was being invaded by materialism and antireligious indoctrination. Quite an undertaking! Lewis was also inevitably influenced by World War II. Finally, for the "Head" idea, Lewis read by chance in a German newspaper of an experiment to keep a dog's head alive by artificial means. His diary even describes a dream he had of a scientist trying to make a corpse immortal by keeping it conscious and its motor nerves alive. Similar experiments were also being performed by Charles Lindbergh.

Because of this diverse range of sources and themes, many critics believed the book was too long. Pan and Avon Books thus both issued abridged versions of the book under the title *The Tortured Planet,* while versions we have today from Macmillan are the original longer edition. No one knows why Lewis allowed an abridged form to be published or details of the arrangement. *The Tortured Planet* contains an abbreviated preface in which Lewis writes: "In reducing the original story to a length suitable for this edition, I believe that I have altered nothing but the tempo and the manner. I myself prefer the more leisurely pace." The original was shortened by more than one-third. But not only did he omit occasional words, many phrases, clauses, whole sentences, and even paragraphs, but he left out many details which develop character and contribute to our understanding of background and themes (e.g., Jane's choice of dissertation topic, description of Bragdon Wood and its history, description of Edgestow, Merlin's history, the mice episode, Filostrato's view of the moon, Mark's reactions to the Head and thoughts about death, Dimble's questioning of his treatment of Mark, and so on). Fortunately, the original unabridged version is the only one available today. And thus the trilogy was completed and in the public's hands.

As you can see, Lewis's inspiration for his novels is wide-ranging. Although it is always difficult to pinpoint any one source, it is certain that the mythology he has created is his own. Although it is rooted firmly in the biblical story of man's fall, Lewis strips it of its "stained-glass and Sunday school" form and gives his myth a unique form, embellishing it with creations from hrossa and sorns to floating islands. They are described so vividly that Lewis must have had a very clear picture of them in his mind. Since the history of Deep Heaven is set forth bit by bit throughout the entire trilogy, we will next examine it, as well as Lewis's planetary creations.

CHAPTER 2: THE MYTH OF DEEP HEAVEN

Never did He make two things the same;
never did He utter one word twice. After
earths, not better earths but beasts; after
beasts, not better beasts, but spirits. After a
falling, not a recovery but a new creation.
Out of the new creation, not a third but the
mode of change itself is changed for ever.
Blessed is He!

The Myth

Lewis's myth is told gradually throughout his stories. This is the history of the Field of Arbol:

Maleldil the Young, who lives with the Old One—a spirit with no body or passions—first made and ruled the world. Each planet was given an Oyarsa, an angelic spirit, to rule. During the years before there was life on earth, the Oyarsa of earth, who was brighter and greater than all the Oyeresu, became "bent" (evil) and these years were thus called the Bent Years. He not only wanted to be like Maleldil, but also decided to destroy other worlds. So with his left hand he smote the moon, so that one side turned away forever from Deep Heaven and toward earth.

Then he tried to invade Malacandra, a planet older than earth. Once the air was warm and full of birdlike creatures, but he robbed it of its atmosphere, bringing cold death on the *harandra,* or high land. (Malacandrians depict this event in their history as a fantastic hnakralike figure in the sky shooting at them with darts.) The planet thus suffered a sort of "fall" in the battle between Maleldil and the Bent Oyarsa. But Maleldil opened up the *handramits* (low ground) to release warm springs and prevent total death of the planet. According to Malacandrian history, Oyarsa made the furrows, the pfifltriggi dug to enlarge them, sorns piled the earth in pinnacles on both sides, and hrossa made the water channels. So the *handramits,* canyons, or, as we see them, "canals" of Mars were engineered by group effort of all its creatures.

Although Malacandra was protected from evil, it is to some extent fallen and now dying. Lewis believed that there may be different sorts and degrees of fallenness. Malacandrians thus have no understanding of concepts of badness, deceitfulness, malice, war, slavery, prostitution, and revenge. When the Bent Oyarsa tried to make the inhabitants of Malacandra see death approaching and fear it and make spaceships for invading other planets, Maleldil stopped them. They now do not fear death, but welcome it. But birds are extinct, the icecaps frozen, and the forests stone. Its "fall" was therefore different than that on earth. In "The Seeing Eye," Lewis says if there are other creatures in the universe they are either: innocent and needing no redemption; both good and bad, redeemed by God in some other way than on earth; needing redemption; or diabolical. Lewis seems to be exploring these first two possibilities in *Perelandra* and *Out of the Silent Planet.*

Eldila are the intermediaries between Oyarsa, who rules the planet, and the three "hnau," or rational species with spirits. Lewis says this "angelocracy" is a thing of the past; only in ancient worlds do we find creatures like those of Malacandra, because the incarnation changed everything. Since Maleldil took on the form of a man, reason must be in human form.

During the Great War which followed the invasion of Malacandra, Maleldil drove the Oyarsa of earth out of the heavens and bound him in the air of earth. Confined to this region below the moon are both he and those eldila who sold themselves to him and have made earth their headquarters. Earth is thus under a state of siege, an "enemy-occupied territory" cut off from the rest of Deep Heaven. Since no message comes from it, it is called the silent planet by all the Oyeresu. Yet because of the evil that grew on earth, there Maleldil "dared terrible things" when he became a man.

Now the Bent Oyarsa, wanting to make war again on Deep Heaven, plans an attack on Perelandra, but can only act through a human agent. Since Perelandra is the youngest of planets, its history is only beginning. It was the first world to waken after the coming of Christ and therefore has no eldila; it is not fallen, but open to temptation. Lewis believed that if there are other rational species, it is not necessary to believe they have fallen. When Perelandra arose from Arbol, the Perelandrian Oyarsa "rounded" the planet, spun air about it, wove its roof, and built the floating islands.

Since the King and Green Lady resist evil, they are given the planet to rule from Tai Harendrimar by their Oyarsa, although he will remain as counsel. When they ascend the throne, it is said that the "world is born" because for the first time two humans have actually gained Paradise. They now have a new and joyful relationship with angels and Nature. With no sense of passing time, they take charge of the seasons and growth, as well as the land, rivers, and beasts. They are to name all creatures, guide all natures to perfection, love all, and bear children. As in Narnia, nobler beasts will become "hnau" and speak. A temple will also be built to Maleldil's glory on the Fixed Land.

The year in which *That Hideous Strength* takes place

(sometime after World War II) is prophesied to be one of great stirrings and changes, for the celestial year which began in the twelfth century is a revolutionary year. Lurga (Saturn) will descend in this age. He is the god of death, cold, and age, and when he visits St. Anne's, those in the house feel the sun dying, the earth gripped in cold, the "heat-death" of the universe, then the blackness of nonentity. For the universe, says Lewis, has been at war—earth's evil eldila warring against those of Deep Heaven—but the siege is now drawing to an end, the two sides becoming more defined. In *Mere Christianity*, Lewis writes that the universe is in "a civil war, a rebellion," and "we are living in a part of the universe occupied by the rebel. Enemy-occupied territory—that is what the world is. Christianity is the story of how the rightful king has landed, you might say landed in disguise, and is calling us all to take part in a great campaign of sabotage."

The "rightful king" is Maleldil. According to the "Seventh Law," Maleldil promised that he would not send powers to mar or mend earth until the end times. Consequently, the dark eldila, knowing there was a barrier at the moon's orbit, confidently believed earth was blockaded from powers of Deep Heaven reaching earth. But when men such as Weston and Devine began sending spaceships to spread sin to other planets, they broke Maleldil's law, opening up a new relationship between men and Maleldil. Now the eldila from Deep Heaven are free to invade earth. But they can only work through the agency of men such as Merlin, whose mind is to be taken over, and Ransom, an intermediary between Heaven and earth. The whole history of earth has led up to the crucial moments described in *That Hideous Strength*. If man shakes off the limitations of his powers imposed by mercy from the results of the fall in the Garden of Eden, Hell will reign incarnate. Evil men will then have the power of evil spirits, making Nature their slave.

Maleldil does not make worlds to live forever. Thus, after Perelandra has made 10,000 revolutions around the sun, the "sky curtain" will be torn down and the Perelandrians will at last see Deep Heaven and be free. Their bodies will take on eldilic form, and some of them, as well as the King, the Malacandrian Oyarsa, and former hnau of earth, will come to earth to participate in its liberation. Earth will then be in final siege and its "black spot" cleared away. Maleldil himself will make war on earth, breaking the moon, then blotting out its light and casting the fragments into the seas so that the smoke shall arise and cover up the sun. There will be plagues and horrors. Yet all will ultimately be cleansed so that the memory of the Black Oyarsa is erased forever and earth can be at last reunited to the Field of Arbol, its real name heard again. This then will be earth's true beginning.

To develop his mythology, Lewis created two unique worlds, complete with their own flora and fauna, histories, social structures, and inhabitants. So vividly detailed are the landscapes that it is apparent Lewis had a very concrete picture in his mind around which he could draw his story.

Malacandra

Even though scientists have recently taken close-up pictures of Mars, we still think of the planet as red with ice-caps and canals. Mars has always been believed to be a warlike planet, older than earth, with flat highlands, dust storms, red vegetation, and desiccation. Lewis keeps much of this tradition in his own description of Malacandra. From a distance, it is the characteristic reddish-yellow disk blotched with greenish blue and capped with white at the poles. Lewis says when he put canals on Mars he already knew this idea had been dissipated by telescopes, but they were part of the traditional myth in the public mind. Older than either earth or Venus, Malacandra is now dying; thus its subdued colors are appropriate. Lewis accounts for other aspects of its appearance with his own details of its geography.

Malacandra is lighter than earth, and since it is farther from the sun, its time is twice as long as ours. The sky is pale blue, the air cold and thin. An abundance of edible weeds resilient as rubber creates a pale pink ground. Actually, there are two types of ground: *handramits* and *harandras*. The *handramits*, engineered when the high ground was smote by the Bent Oyarsa of earth and thus made uninhabitable, are geometrically shaped—some parallel, some intersecting, some triangular. Appearing as purple lines or "canals" from above, they are really engineered canyons of lowland where the warmth and air are located. The purplish effect is created by vegetables with soft, flimsy, forty-foot stalks and leaves like transparent lifeboats! Blue effervescent water of the *handramits* descends with high and narrow waves into tepid, blue, hissing gullies and streams. Between the *handramits* is flat, airless, lifeless waste, created mainly by the old forests of Malacandra. Once alive with birds, they are now petrified masses of pale rose, tinted, stone "cauliflowers" the size of cathedrals. The *harandras,* or high ground, are rose-red, a world of naked, faintly green rock interspersed with patches of red. There the air is thinner and colder, the light brighter and sky darker, than below. Mountains are greenish white and shaped like pylons with haphazard grouping and irregular shapes, such as points, knobs, or rough platforms.

To the north and east are the sand deserts of Malacandra, which appear as yellow and ochre. Windstorms raise the sand in a dull, red cloudlike mass to heights of over seventeen feet. West are the forest lowlands, where the pfifltriggi live and which on earth appear as the dark patches of Mars. But these are actually the old, greenish blue oceans of the planet.

Overall, the landscape thus appears as a pastel, water-color picture of purplish and whitish-green fringed by rose-colored, cloudlike masses. Gorges· appear as purple, blue, yellow and pinkish white created by the mixture of woodland and water. But perhaps the most striking thing about Malacandra—as if all this were not unusual enough—is the fact that everything is perpendicular: narrow and pointed at the top, small at the base, elongated from the natural effect of lesser gravity. Ransom sees this "rush to the sky" or "skyward impulse" as symbolic of an aspiration toward God. Once home, he also finds it hard to forget the perpetual singing and the special smells of the planet—an aromatic, spicy, cold, thin tingle at the back of your nose.

Meldilorn, where the Oyarsa dwells, is a particularly striking spot on Malacandra reminiscent of a paradisal earth. Ransom first comes upon it as gray, seemingly "downland" ridges rising and falling like sea waves into a blue-gray valley. In the midst of it lies a twelve-mile-wide, circular sapphire lake bordered by purple forest. A red pyramid of island rises like a jewel from the water and glimmers with huge golden flowers as tall as trees. Appropriate for the dwelling-place of a ruler is the special quality of depth, dimness, and softness in the landscape. From the monoliths lining the long avenue, Ransom learns a bit about the history of Malacandra, its place in the solar system, and of its three strange species of creatures.

The only animal life we meet on Malacandra are pale, furry creatures somewhat like giraffes, only slenderer and higher. But there are three distinct, rational beings—hrossa, sorns, and pfifltriggi—seemingly representative of the various kinds of fauna on earth—animal, bird, and reptile/insect.

The *hrossa* are a combination of seal, otter, and penguin. They are slender and flexible, six to seven feet high, with thick, hairy black coats like a seal's. Their round, heavily whiskered heads have high foreheads, small laughing mouths, and glistening amber eyes. Their short legs are webbed, as are their strong clawed arms, and the tail is like a beaver's or fish's. Although these are the predominant characteristics of most hrossa, a few white hrossa exist, as well as the ten-foot black and silver hrossa who dwell in the west and are dancers.

As Ransom learns and loves so well firsthand, the hrossa live in the *handramits* near the rivers in beehive-shaped huts made of stiff leaves. Their culture might be considered stone-age since they sleep on the ground, use stone knives and primitive vessels, and eat only fish and boiled vegetables, for they are great fishermen and farmers. Yet the hrossa are talented speakers, singers, and poets. Like the

Anglo-Saxons, they perform their poetry and music by a team of four hrossa: one chants while the others interpret with song. But because they believe the writing of books destroys poetry, they unfortunately now have fewer books. Their humor is extravagant and fantastic.

Ransom is surprised that hrossa are monogamous, limiting their breeding to once in a lifetime and a couple of offspring. To them, sex is not a separate act from procreation, but a totality. They have a normal temperature of 103 degrees, live 160 years, and marry at 40. Lewis felt that he made their birth rate a bit too slow, but was picturing their world in extreme old age, like an "old man tranquilly or happily proceeding to his end." In addition, Ransom adds, they don't cry tears or blink, and their inoffensive droppings are used for fertilizer.

Lewis says his "dear friends the hrossa" are theologians, in a sense, because they know the Old One (God) and Maleldil (Christ). However, they do not know the Third One (Holy Spirit) because they have never fallen, "thence never been redeemed, thence never baptized, thence never received the gift of the Holy Ghost."

While those on earth fear death because of the fall, the hrossa see it as entering a better world through spiritual rebirth into a life with Maleldil. Each who dies naturally dies at a predictable time (160 earth years), when his full lifespan is over. Then the body is in a sense "unmade" or unbodied, scattered into nothing during the burial ceremony. They describe this as dropping the body into a still pool so the hnau can rise from the body into a second life.

Of all the hnau, *sorns* are the most like men, yet closest to the traditional "science fiction" outer space creature pictured on pulp magazines. Over two to three times the height of a man, sorns are white, spindly, flimsy, and "madly elongated." The heads are narrow and conical; the faces are thin and unnaturally long with a solemn, severe, almost human expression, eyes that seem too small, and either a cream-colored beard or double chin. The thin, mobile, spidery, and almost transparent hands are fan-shaped, with seven fingers covered with skin over the bone like a bird's. (Perhaps they are the vestige of the bird-life that once flourished in the *harandras*.) Similarly, their thin, elongated legs lift their feet high and set them down gently, so that they glide with almost a skating motion at right angles to the slopes. Thus all movements in general are spidery. The body itself tops in a heavily pouted chest and ends in long, wedge-shaped buttocks. A soft, featherlike substance that reflects the light provides a natural coat all the way down to the ankles.

Sorns have a solitary life in individual caves dotting the *harandras*. As the "intellectuals" of the planet, they are interested in such things as astromony and history and hopelessly inept at boating, fishing, swimming, and creating or understanding poetry. Perhaps that is why Lewis calls them "sorns," which means "those who depend on others for existence" (*Oxford English Dictionary*). Their language, called *Surnibur*, is spoken in booming voices. Compared to the other Malacandrian hnau, their humor is ironic and females are of less importance.

Pfifltriggi are the nervous and amusing frog-, insect-, reptilelike creatures of Malacandra. Their long, pointed, yellow, shabby, hairless faces have low foreheads, long snouts, and a heavy development at the back and behind the ears. The entire head can swivel around like a mantis's, while the dry, rasping noise made when they move is like a grasshopper. The pfifltrigg who busily chisels Ransom's portrait is arrayed in a light, scaly, richly decorated substance and has furry folds draped around his neck like a comforter, in addition to chains around both neck and limbs!

These creatures dwell within the old ocean beds of Malacandra in the lush blue and green forests and warm mines, in houses with many pillars and paintings. With their delicate and many-fingered hands, they dig and make crafts— things both useful and beautiful, nonuseful, and the intricate objects designed by the sorns. This artwork is often created out of stone with elaborate ornamentation, a mixture of pure

line drawings, designs, and packed and empty surfaces. Through their art they keep the historical records of the planet as well.

Unlike the other hnau, the pfifltriggi are shorter-lived, oviparous, and matriarchal, so their females are very important. Their humor, in contrast to that of the others, is sharp and excelling in abuse. They are the only Malacandrians who enjoy Devine's tobacco!

Perelandra

Venus has always been considered younger and warmer than earth. It was pictured as watery, with tall mountains and thick, vaporous clouds which serve as a barrier between it and the heavens.

Again, Perelandra combines these traditional qualities with others so unique that Ransom finds something there "that might overload a human brain." The sky seems distant and golden because of the cloud cover so thick that it reflects light, producing a riot of colors in the atmosphere and an impenetrable darkness at night. Unlike Malacandra's pastel world, the colors of Perelandra are heraldic. Tepid and "delicately gorgeous" gold, green, and blue waves rise like columns. Inhabiting their depths are a multitude of phosphorescent creatures right out of the pages of mythology: eels, darting things in armor, heraldic sea horses, seal-centaurs, dragons, mermaids, and the silvery, dolphinlike fish that can propel you quickly through the water. Other inhabitants of Perelandra, all content in their submission to the King and Green Lady, are huge pigeon- and flame-colored birds, stork-like birds, dragons, rat-sized beaverlike creatures, short-legged and elongated pigs, and vividly colored "frogs" that rain down from the heavens.

On the waters float multicolored (flame, ultramarine, orange, gamboge, violet) islands of heatherlike vegetable matter. Due to the action of the waves, these islands change shape constantly, creating perpetually new landscapes of hills, valleys, forests, and feathery vegetation tall as gooseberries and the color of sea anemones. The "globe trees," which provide Ransom such a special unearthly pleasure, have gray and purple tubelike trunks with yellow globes of fruit perched amid splashes of oranges, silvers, and blues.

While the floating islands fill just part of the oceans, sometimes separate, sometimes forming one huge aggregate of matter, there is also a "Fixed Land" on which the King and Queen are forbidden to spend the night. This is a mountainous island with a smooth coast, valleys, and mountainy pillars or crags rising in green columns of bluish turf. Nine piers of rock near the center form a sort of circle surrounding a seven-acre oval plateau of fine turf and crimson flowers. At first Ransom rejoices in the stability of the land, the trees so much like those of earth, and the silent, cool, dark atmosphere. Yet after just one restless and uncomfortable night, he again longs for the floating islands and their more pleasurable fruits and fragrant breezes.

On his chase with the Un-man over the seemingly endless expanses of water, Ransom realizes how little of the planet he has seen or has ever been seen by any eyes, and how many creatures may exist not solely for man's benefit. Suddenly he and the Un-man are swept through a hole in a cliff into a cavern of total darkness. Within the layer upon layer of caves he discovers a subterranean fire and insectlike inhabitants with their own ancient halls and chambers, government, and forms of worship. At first horrible to Ransom, one of these creatures becomes to him "a mantled form, huge and still and slender . . . with insufferable majesty," and he again feels like an intruder.

When Ransom emerges from this "cave of ice," he finds himself on another "fixed land." Though it is blanketed off and on in mists, he can catch occasional glimpses of vast, flower-dotted mountain slopes. He contentedly climbs ever upward toward the Holy Mountain where the coronation ceremony for the King and Queen takes place. Under ripple-trees (two and a half foot trees with blue streamers) graze tiny mountain "mice" the size of bumblebees. At last he comes upon dazzling translucent crystal cliffs, their peaks immersed in red flowers. The rose-red valley at their center contains a small pool edged with lilies. This is the paradisal fixed land where the throne of the King and Queen will be and for which the other Fixed Land, by their obedience, prepared them. This is Lewis's portrait of what will happen when we, too, are given the Morning Star.

Lewis's planetary creations come not only from tradition and from elements in his own vast imagination, but also from an even more elaborate picture that comes to us from the Middle Ages. Lewis was a scholar of medieval literature and culture, drawing on their metaphors for the universe, as we shall see next.

CHAPTER 3: MEDIEVAL PERSPECTIVES AND THE TRILOGY

Not as when stones lie side by side, but as
when stones support and are supported in an
arch, such is His order. . . . In the plan of
the Great Dance plans without number
interlock, and each movement becomes in its
season the breaking into flower of the whole
design to which all else had been directed.

Although Lewis creates his own "myth" which totally renews our way of looking at things, much of his material is actually rooted in the ancient medieval way of seeing life. This medieval background of the trilogy restores in us a belief about man and the heavens which existed 300 or 400 years ago and which we have sadly lost. Lewis's explanation of these concepts can be found in his key book on medieval and Renaissance literature, *The Discarded Image,* and in his essay "Imagination and Thought in the Middle Ages" in his book *Studies in Medieval and Renaissance Literature.* While the medieval model illustrated a belief in the order of space, the

Arthurian legend, as will be discussed in the next chapter, reflected an order on earth.

The medieval model of the universe showed it to be large and of a perfect spherical shape. The round earth stood motionless at the center, surrounded by a series of seven hollow, transparent globes, one about the other, each larger, quicker, more powerful than the one below. Fixed in each of the seven spheres was one luminous body: the lowest, slowest, and smallest was the moon; then came Mercury, Venus, the Sun, Mars, Jupiter, Saturn, and the sphere of the Fixed Stars *(Stellatum)*. The next sphere, called the Primum Mobile or First Mover, was a sphere of pure, intellectual light and caused all to rotate through love for God and imitation of him. Beyond all this was the infinite "Empyrean," or true Heaven. Lewis emphasizes that while the earth was central, it was really insignificant, merely a point.

Lewis's idea in the trilogy that the Bent Archon of earth was bound in the air of earth and confined to the region below the moon with his evil eldila (or eldils) also draws on a medieval concept. From Aristotle came the idea that the moon's orbit is a boundary (like a city wall) between two regions of the universe. Everything below the moon ("Region of Air") was irregular, mutable, perishable, and subject to luck, decay, and death; everything above the moon ("Aether") was perfect, constant, regular, and eternal. The region of Heaven above the Empyrean was pure, divine substance.

This scheme was not only simple and perfect, but seen as strictly ordered, like a building or finished work that could evoke charm and wonder. Whereas we see such a model as perhaps ridiculous and such regularity as monotonous, medieval man saw the heavens as free because they are so planned and mapped out.

Carved in stone is the similar Malacandrian picture of the universe, which begins with a segment of a circle filled with Malacandrian scenes. Behind and above this is three-fourths of a disk divided into concentric rings which revolve around the sun (Arbol) at the center. On each ring is a little ball holding a winged angel: first Mercury (Viritrilbia), portrayed with wings and a trumpet signifying his role as messenger of the gods; then Venus (Perelandra), shown as a female figure. Earth (Thulcandra) comes next, but its angel (Lucifer, the Black Archon) is erased. So, as Ransom learns later, earth is a mere "black spot" in the universe whose Oyarsa or planetary angel is not only evil, but whose real history has not even begun. The fourth circle of Mars touches the top of the segment of Malacandrian scenes and comes in toward the spectator. Jupiter (Glundandra) is considered the King, greatest of worlds, the real center of all. Ransom says the Malacandrians thus turn the solar system inside-out. To them, the asteroids are Dancers on the edge of the planets or Great Worlds; Jupiter is the "center," as in ancient mythology, for it is associated with something of "vast importance." For this reason, the Oyarsa tells Ransom, earthlings must drop out of Heaven *into* a world because earth is outside Heaven; space is the realm of myth and light.

Lewis turns our own view of the universe inside-out by explaining how even the Ptolemaic model with earth at the center should really be turned around. For the *spatial* order is quite the opposite of the *spiritual*. The physical cosmos, in other words, "mirrors" or reverses spiritual reality; so what is truly the rim seems to us the hub. In actuality, the bent and silent earth is at the edge of all life: "All this time we are describing the universe spread out in space; dignity, power and speed progressively diminishing as we descend from its circumference to its centre, the Earth. But I have already hinted that the intelligible universe reverses it all; there the Earth is the rim, the outside edge where being fades away on the border of nonentity. A few astonishing lines from the *Paradiso* . . . stamp this on the mind forever." In a better model—like that of Dante—if we moved outward through the planets to space, we would see seven concentric circles revolving around a point. These are the various orders of angels circling around God as the center of light. Although the earth has no place in this "dance," it is drawn in by the end of Dante's poem. This turning inside-out is, in a way, a symbol for Dante's spiritual conversion, involving a choice of God rather than the Devil.

What Lewis is, of course, saying is that while the ancient model was physically teleocentric and anthropocentric, it was spiritually theocentric. In other words, this spatial metaphor illustrates the spiritual universe where God, not man, is at the center. Being bent by sin, earth is thus cut off from and outside the universe. Lewis encounters this same phenomenon in *The Great Divorce* as he climbs in a bus going to Heaven. He has a sense of being in a large space, but also of having gotten "out" of earth "in some sense which made the Solar System itself seem an indoor affair." Whereas we feel like we are looking *out* at a cold, dark, starry night sky, in this inverted perspective we would be looking *into* a world filled with revelry and love. Thus, the heavenly bodies do not move in a pitch-black vacuum. According to medieval theory, darkness is caused simply by the long, conical shadow cast by earth when the sun is below our feet. Beyond, the heavens are bright and resonant, bathed in a perpetual sunshine. Lewis writes: "In modern, that is, in evolutionary, thought man stands at the top of a stair whose foot is lost in obscurity; in this, he stands at the bottom of a stair whose top is invisible" with warmth and light.

God, not earth, is the center of this "spiritual" model. At the end of *Perelandra,* the eldila sing that Maleldil "is the centre. Because we are with Him, each of us is at the centre. . . . Each is equally at the centre. . . . There seems no centre because it is all centre." God is the source and creator of all that exists, "the opaque centre of all existences."

Not only did the medieval model use the circle as a metaphor for the universe because of its association with perfection and wholeness, but the circle has been used for centuries as a symbol for God. The definition of God as a sphere "whose center is everywhere and circumference nowhere" provides an excellent symbol for both eternity and immensity and probably began as early as the twelfth century. All points on the sphere are equal to each other and joined to the center; the center is both fixed and eternal, yet at harmony with and encompassing all things because action from the center causes all points to exist.

Naturally, Weston's model of the universe is the depressing opposite of the medieval model. He argues that the good things in life are like a thin little rind or outer skin of life "put on for show, and then—the *real* universe for ever and ever." The dead descend into the "inner darkness: under the rind. All witless, all twittering, gibbering, decaying. . . . Picture the universe as an infinite globe with this very thin crust on the outside. But remember its thickness is a thickness of *time*. It's about seventy years thick in the best places. We are born on the surface of it and all our lives we are sinking through it. When we've got all the way through we are what's called Dead: we've got into the dark part inside, the real globe. If your God exists, He's not in the globe—He's outside, like a moon. As we pass into the interior we pass out of His ken. He doesn't follow us in. . . . He's not in time. . . . He stays put: out in the light and air, outside. . . . From His point of view, we move *away*, into what He regards as nonentity, where He never follows." But in *The Problem of Pain*, Lewis says it is Hell which is "the darkness outside," the "outer rim where being fades away into nonentity."

Since earth is alone, outside the heavens, no message comes from it. Yet because the universe is like a web, traces of the history of the universe are still alive in its memory. In turn, it has unfortunately involved the whole cosmos in its fall. Earth is described as being under the "crushing weight of terrestrial gravity" (sin): "the shadow of one dark wing is over all Tellus." It has no Oyarsa "because every one of them wants to be a little Oyarsa himself." We are also shown as being completely out of kilter to God and the heavens. For example, earth seems upside-down when viewed from Mars, and the Oyeresu have such a totally different plane of refer-

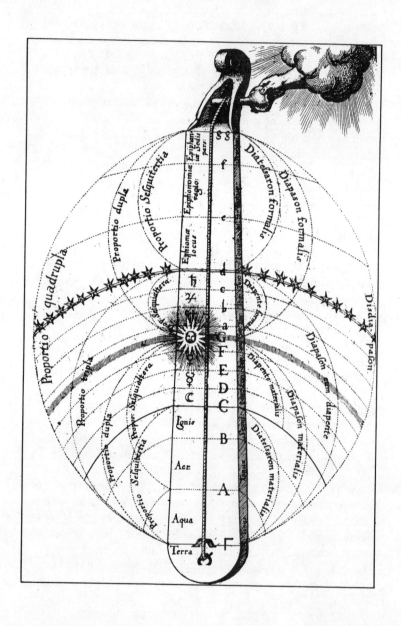

ence that they make everything around them seem aslant.

The Music of the Spheres

The Music of the Spheres is another medieval description of the universe used frequently in ancient writers, as well as in modern writers such as Lewis, J. R. R. Tolkien, and Madeleine L'Engle. According to the Pythagorean model, the sun, moon, and planets revolve in concentric circles around the earth, each fastened to a sphere or wheel. They are aligned in such exact mathematical relationships and revolve at such constant speeds that each creates sound waves, proportionate to its speed of orbit, as it moves through space. Each planet sings one note, creating one, never-ending chord. Thus the orbits, as in the illustration, were pictured as a huge lyre or violin with strings curved in circles, tuned by the hand of God, and creating a symphony of sound. The Platonists believed that the music was created by the singing of the Intelligences who sat on each sphere.

When Johannes Kepler, a seventeenth century astronomer, learned that the planets move in elliptical, not circular, paths with different speeds, he calculated the changing speeds, size, and shape of each planet to determine what tone each gave off. According to his theory, the Music of the Spheres was a continuous but ever-changing song.*

Thus, the men of the Middle Ages did not think space dead and silent, but rather filled perpetually with sweet sound, "a vast, lighted concavity filled with music and life." We on earth cannot hear the music, they said, for two reasons: because of the fall (sin) and because it is too familiar to us to be heard. In his poem "The Ecstasy," Lewis says there is a constant, dull, relentless rhythm beneath Nature's surface even though the "permanent background" has failed our ears.

*Professors at Yale have recently used computers and synthesizers to record the sounds Kepler predicted. In their simulation, Mercury whistles like a shrill piccolo, Venus hums, Earth moans, Mars sings a fast-moving tune with a wide range of tones, Uranus ticks, Neptune clicks, and Jupiter thumps! (*Cincinnati Enquirer*, May 6, 1979, K-8)

Another medieval diagram of the universe gives us a possible source for Lewis's idea of fallen earth as the "silent" planet. Apollo, or God, is envisioned as enthroned in Heaven; beneath him plunges to earth a serpent. There are eight strings, eight musical modes, and eight celestial spheres. But earth makes nine—one too many—thus destroying the perfection of the scheme. In *Survival of the Pagan Gods,* a book Lewis refers to several times in *The Discarded Image,* we learn that in 1518 Gafurio, basing this theory on Cicero, corrected this little inconsistency by declaring that earth, being motionless, was therefore silent. So earth's Muse (Thalia) does not take part in the Music of the Spheres. Lewis, of course, explains that it is the sin brought upon Thulcandra by the Bent Archon that causes it to be silent; the Oyarsa no longer communicates with the other Oyeresu.

Tolkien uses the idea of God creating the universe, not just through his Word, but also through Song, at the beginning of *The Silmarillion.* Eru (God) creates the Ainor, or Holy Ones, as offsprings of his thought as musical themes. Their singing before him in harmony creates a Great Music, whereas evil and proud beings sing their own music, creating discord. As Screwtape says, Noise is the devils' only defense against the music, melodies, and silences of God's universe. In contrast, when Ransom is triumphant in winning one of many arguments against the Un-man and thus in holding the Green Lady a bit longer from temptation, he hears "festal revelry and dance and splendour poured into him—no sound, yet in such fashion that it could not be remembered or thought of except as music. . . . It was like being present when the morning stars sang together." He even describes himself as an instrument which he hopes is tuned up to concert pitch.

In *The Magician's Nephew,* Aslan also appropriately sings Narnia into creation with a beautiful noise formed from ideas in his own mind. There is also an obvious connection between the notes Aslan sings and the things created, for each species has its own notes. But to create this glorious harmony, each thing must, in turn, create its own tune, contributing to the majestic whole. Lewis writes: "If all experienced God in the same way and returned Him an identical worship, the song of the Church triumphant would have no symphony, it would be like an orchestra in which all the instruments played the same note." At the end of his Perelandrian journey, Ransom notices that while the King is God's live image made by divine artistry, he is "a copy, like and not the same, an echo, a rhyme, an exquisite reverberation of the uncreated music prolonged in a created medium." And in the final ceremony, the multitude of transcorporeal intelligences and beasts form an enclosed circle, "and with their coming all the separate notes of strength or beauty which that assembly had hitherto struck became one music."

The Great Dance

Just as the created universe was an act of and in a state of music, it was also believed to be in a perpetual dance. Like the music metaphor, the dance was used by mystics and poets like Dante, Sir John Davies, and Milton to show the harmony, order, freedom, and measured movement of the universe. The medieval picture of the Intelligence of the *Primum Mobile* was a girl gaily dancing and playing the tambourine. Many cults also believed that any pomp on earth reflects this dance in order to participate in it and bring about the union of God and man. Later, however, Newton and Galileo destroyed these ideas by declaring that the universe runs more like a machine.

At the end of the song of the eldila, Ransom is granted a vision of this Dance: "It seemed to be woven out of the intertwining undulation of many cords or bands of light, leaping over and under one another and mutually embraced in arabesques and flower-like subtleties. . . . Particles were the secular generalities of which history tells—people, institutions, climates of opinion, civilizations, arts, sciences, and the like—ephemeral coruscations that piped their short song and vanished. The ribbons or cords . . . were individual entities. . . . Some of the thinner and more delicate cords were beings that we call short-lived: flowers and insects, a fruit or a storm of rain, and once (he thought) a wave of the sea. Others were such things as we also think lasting: crystals, rivers, mountains, or even stars. . . . Some were universal truths or universal qualities." When the King and Queen and all the creatures laugh, "new modes of joy that had nothing to do with mirth as we understand it passed into them all, as it were from the very air, or as if there were dancing in Deep Heaven. Some say there always is."

Likewise, as the gods descend on St. Anne's, those present feel as if they are taking their places in the "ordered rhythm of the universe, side by side with punctual seasons and patterned atoms and the obeying Seraphim."

The Dance, as you can see, is an appropriate metaphor for the perfect joy, harmony, and unity of all creation, where every person, animal, plant, and stone plays a vital part. Just as each being produces a precise note that blends into the harmony of the universe, each individual's path is part of the Dance of the whole. And just as evil beings desire to create disharmony and discordant music, so too the temptation is to dance on one's own. In *Mere Christianity*, Lewis writes: "The whole dance, or drama, or pattern of this three-Personal life is to be played out in each of us: or (putting it the other way round) each one of us has got to enter that pattern, take his place in that dance. There is no other way to the happiness for which we were made."

The Great Chain of Being

Individuals were believed to not only have a place in a Dance, but in a "Chain" or hierarchical ladder of beings descending from God and to a vast number of precisely ordered angels, to man, beasts, and finally various inanimate objects. Not only was every particle of creation a link in the Chain, important for its own special role in God's plan, but every step in the ladder was *filled* (this was called "plentitude") with beings. Hierarchy and the belief in divine creatures is central to both Lewis's and Tolkien's mythologies.

The hierarchy of Malacandra is as follows:

> The Old One
> Maleldil the Young
> Oyarsa (tutelary ruler)
> eldila (responsible for creatures)
> hnau
> dumb animals

"There must be rule," says a sorn, "yet how can creatures rule themselves? Beasts must be ruled by hnau and hnau by eldila and eldila by Maleldil." Since Oyarsa rules all, the three hnau (hrossa, sorns, and pfifltriggi) live equally, cooperate with one another, and in fact complement one another (e.g., the gathering of all three produces the best humor). Since each is to the other as both man and animal, the same and yet different, they need no pets and feel differently about "lower" animals than we do. In fact, the sorns pity earth for having only one hnau, which they believe must greatly narrow our sympathies and thought.

On Perelandra the hierarchy is a bit different, since there are no eldila as intermediaries between Maleldil and his people since Christ came to earth:

> The Old One
> Maleldil the Young
> the King
> Green Lady
> animals

Unlike the situation on fallen earth, animals are content being in subjection to the Green Lady, eagerly attending to her while she, in turn, loves and teaches them.

In the final ceremony, the hierarchy is represented by the arrangement of beings on one side of the pool: first eldila; then Ransom; next, the four singing beasts; and finally, the other animals. The King and Queen are called the Keystone of the arch, the bridging of the gap between transcorporeal intelligences and beasts which has existed on earth ever since the fall. At the close of *That Hideous Strength*, however, Perelandra comes to earth to "make men sane" and no longer isolated: "We are now as we ought to be," says Ransom, "between the angels who are our elder brothers and the beasts who are our jesters, servants, and playfellows." With evil temporarily conquered, man occupies his proper place in the Great Chain.

Oyeresu and Eldila

"Longaevai" (long-livers) or angels are real and vital parts of the Chain of Being. According to the medieval model, space was inhabited by an enormous number of intermediaries between man and God who lived between the Empyrean and the moon. So, "Medieval man looked up at a sky not only melodious, sunlit, and splendidly inhabited, but also incessantly active." As the, chart shows, traditionally there were said to be nine classes of angels ranging from seraphim to angels. Aerial demons, like Lewis's Dark Eldila, were believed to live between the moon and earth. Lewis said he wanted to show the rich universe as being full of a variety of creatures different from humans. His eldila, he explained, are angels, not fairies, always about Maleldil's business and whose habitat is space. Good and bad eldila wage a perpetual invisible warfare.

NINE CLASSES OF ANGELS

Name	Orientation	
Seraphim	closest to God	
Cherubim	look God-ward	
Thrones	contemplate Divine essence; unconcerned with created universe; associated with heat, burning	
Dominations	face God with backs to earth	
Virtues	responsible for general order of Nature	
Powers	potentially active	
Principalities	deal with destiny of nations	deal with
Archangels	deal with individuals	human affairs;
Angels		more active

Medieval man believed each planet was controlled by a resident planetary Intelligence or angelic spirit whom Lewis calls an Oyarsa. His responsibility was to keep his sphere moving by desire for God. At the end of *Out of the Silent Planet*, Lewis tells us that he got the name "Oyarsa" from a medieval Platonist, Bernardus Silvestris, whom he refers to frequently in *The Discarded Image*. According to Bernardus, the Oyarsa, or as he spells it, "Usiarch" ("deputed power"), is the "Genius" whom God has given power over natural things and who gives shape to their forms. Lewis's Oyeresu, the greatest of eldila, were put on the planets to rule when they were made and to keep them in their orbits. The Malacandrians depict these Oyeresu as winged flames on each sphere. All Oyeresu speak together, except for earth's, who is silent. But every Oyarsa still has a representative (wraith) on earth, just as in every world there is an unfallen partner of the Black Archon. Thus, in old times, when men reported they had seen gods, it was only these wraiths they had seen. Jane, for example, encounters the buxom earthly wraith of Venus in the lodge, accompanied by her romping and mischievous dwarves.

Earth's Oyarsa (Lucifer), who was brighter and greater than Malacandra's, became bent long before human life began on earth. Although he was free, he desired to spoil other worlds beside his own: "There was great war, and we drove him back out of the heavens and bound him in the air of his own world. . . . There doubtless he lies to this hour," explains Malacandra's Oyarsa.

Lewis probably derived the name *eldil* from the Norwegian *eld* (fire or flame) or Anglo-Saxon *eald* (old, chief) and the Old Norse *engill* (angel). He was also no doubt influenced by Tolkien's *eldar* (type of elves). Ransom compares eldila to our traditional idea of albs, devas, gods, angels, and fairies. Tellurian eldila are a different and hostile kind of eldil who chose to follow the Bent Oyarsa of earth and are thus the reason for the "fatal bent" of earth's whole history.

Angels are traditionally transsexual and wholly intuitive and intellectual—naked minds. The Bible, for example, indicates that angels have no physical bodies, though they may take on visible form, and do not reproduce, marry, age, get sick, or die. Likewise, Malacandra's Oyarsa lives an enormous time, has no sense of duration, and does not die or breed. Though his habitat is space, he abides at Meldilorn and has ruled all hnau and everything in Malacandra since its creation. Like all hnau he is a copy of Maleldil, and like Maleldil he is a "terrible good." Ransom describes him as being like a mere whisper of light—actually, light goes through him—"like a silence spreading over a room full of people, like an infinitesimal coolness on a sultry day, like a passing memory of some long-forgotten sound or scent, like all that is stillest and smallest and most hard to seize in nature." His unearthly, inorganic voice, which most likely works by manipulating the human eardrums, sounds to Ransom as if rock, crystal, or light had spoken. Like Maleldil himself, the Oyarsa is characterized by a weightiness. For if "we must have a mental picture to symbolise Spirit," writes Lewis, "we should represent it as something *heavier* than matter."

Most authorities agree in giving these creatures incredible swiftness and unlimited powers of transformation. Similarly, Lewis's Oyeresu and eldila affect Ransom as a unique and awesome experience. Bernardus Silvestris describes certain angels who are assigned to watch over man and show him "by forebodings of mind, dreams, or portentous displays of external signs, the dangers to be avoided. The divinity of these beings is not wholly simple or pure, for it is enclosed in a body, albeit an ethereal one. . . . Since their bodies are virtually incorporeal, and subtler than those of lower creatures, though coarser than those of higher powers, the feeble perception of man is unable to apprehend them."

Similarly, Ransom has difficulty in describing the size and shape of the bodies of eldila, "hnau" of superior intelligence. They have bodies, but we cannot see them because light simply goes right through them: "the body of an eldil is a movement swift as light; you might say its body is made of light, but not of that which is light for the eldil. His 'light' is a swifter movement which for us is nothing at all; and what we call light is for him . . . a thing he can touch and bathe in. . . . What we call firm things—flesh and earth—seem to him thinner, and harder to see than our light, and more like clouds, and nearly nothing. To us the eldil is a thin, half-real body that can go through walls and rocks: to himself he goes through them because he is solid and firm and they are like cloud." So, to Ransom's eye they appear only as "footsteps of light," variations of light and shade like a sunbeam or moving of the leaves. To his ear their voices seem a silvery sound. Conscious of his humanity, Ransom feels embarrassed and shy in their presence.

Lewis says that if angels (whom he believes are actual beings) have that relation to pagan gods as they have in Perelandra, then they might really manifest themselves in their real form. Thus, the Oyeresu of Malacandra and Perelandra, by affecting Ransom's retina, appear to him in a variety of visible forms. Malacandra's Oyarsa seems like a pillar or rod of light of indescribable color. The two Oyeresu turn into a tornado of monstrosities—darting pillars filled with eyes, lightning pulsations of flame, talons, beaks, billowy snowlike masses, cubes, and heptagons. Next, they become concentric wheels turning inside each other. Both of these descriptions are very similar to Ezekiel's description of cherubim in the Bible (Ezekiel, chapters 1 and 10); they too are characterized by flashes and pulses of lightning, glowing wheels with rims edged with eyes.

Finally, the two Oyeresu become thirty-foot undulating naked bodies with long, sparkling hair and one changeless, pure expression of spiritual, intellectual love. They are an opaque burning white but translucent around the edges, with unearthly colors flashing about their shoulders, neck and faces like plumage or halos. Seeming to rush toward Ransom at great speed, they are not vertical, but make it seem as if the valley is at an angle, for they are moving in *their* world. While Malacandra is cold, metallic, pure, hard, and the colors of morning, Perelandra has the warm colors of vegetable life.

These two beings reveal to Ransom the *real* meaning of gender. Gender, he realizes, is a reality and has nothing to do with sex, but rather a "fundamental polarity." Lewis was aware of the Greek doctrine that Form is masculine, Matter feminine, and therefore the relation between creator and created is the relation between male and female. So God, who is "above and beyond all things is so masculine that we are all feminine in relation to it." Mars or Ares is a rhythm, the quantitative; Venus or Aphrodite, a melody and accentual meter. While Mars stands vigilant with spear in hand, Venus' eyes open inward to a land of waves and fragrant, dewy air like the planet itself, and her palms are open toward Ransom.

Lewis follows carefully the traditional characteristics of all the gods of the planets who descend to earth. Each creates in the humans at St. Anne's the mood, abilities, and impulses which he controls. For example, Viritrilbia (Mercury), the god of language, produces in the group the ability to speak puns, metaphors, and witty sayings; Ransom can even see into the "white-hot furnace" of language itself. Malacandra (Mars), the god of war, makes those in the house suddenly yearn to recklessly combat the forces of Belbury or dream of great historical battles. Perelandra (Venus), the goddess of love, brings on such a sweet, drowsy warmth and amorous atmosphere that eventually every creature in the area—even bumbling Mr. Bultitude—seeks his mate. Lurga (Saturn), who is to descend in this age, gives the members a foretaste of the coldness, death, and nothingness which will accompany the end times. Finally, Jupiter the King sends the group into a festal, leaping dance of joy, laughter, pomp, ceremony, and heroic energy.

Eldila rule only in the ancient worlds. Therefore, since Perelandra was the first world created after Christ's incarnation, there are no eldila on that planet. Rather, Maleldil and the two humans communicate directly, with no need for intermediaries. The job of eldila is to cherish and make humans "older" (more knowledgeable and mature) until they are even older than the eldila and the eldila can then fall at their feet. Lewis is here closely following biblical information about man's relationship to angels. Man is created "a little lower than the angels," both physically and intellectually (Hebrews 2:7). Yet the incarnation, crucifixion, and act of atonement of Christ was solely for man's sin, allowing a special relationship between man and God which angels cannot enjoy. Angels have always been available to serve and aid man as messengers of God. But at the future resurrection, man will be made higher than the angels (implied in Luke 20:36).

As you can see, Lewis liked these wonderful ancient ideas about the universe. Medieval theories about the planetary system and metaphors of the Music, the Great Dance, and hierarchy of beings, complete with supernatural creatures, beasts, and even inorganic matter, reflected a belief that there is a carefully and intricately patterned universe crafted by a Divine Artisan. The Arthurian legend, which we shall look at next and which Lewis used as a framework for *That Hideous Strength,* reflects a belief that an order which represents God's rule and harmony with his will can be found here and now on earth.

CHAPTER 4: MYTHOLOGY, ARTHURIAN LEGEND, AND THE TRILOGY

*For though the healing what was wounded
and the straightening what was bent is a new
dimension of glory, yet the straight was not
made that it might be bent nor the whole that
it might be wounded. The ancient peoples are
at the centre. Blessed be He!*

The Legend

Many of the names in *That Hideous Strength* which may seem unfamiliar to you—Logres, Pendragon, Fisher-King, and Merlin—come from the legend of King Arthur, which Lewis very adeptly links to his planetary myth. Like Cecil Dimble, Lewis believed the legend was mostly true history. Most of his material was derived from his friend Charles Williams, who was a member of a literary circle of Lewis's friends called the Inklings. Williams read aloud to Lewis his Arthurian poems called *Taliessin Through Logres* and *The Region of the Summer Stars*. His hero is not King Arthur but the poet Taliessin, who journeys through Britain, Byzantium, and

Logres. Head of a "Company of the Redeemed," he attempts to set up an order in chaotic Logres so the Holy Grail can dwell there. These two poems are very difficult because of their complex symbolism; so Lewis wrote a helpful analysis and commentary on the works which can be found in *Arthurian Torso* ("Williams and the Arthuriad"). Lewis was probably also influenced to some extent by Tennyson's Christianized version of the Arthur legend in *Idylls of the King* (1857-1885).

Dimble, Denniston, and Ransom are said to share a knowledge of Arthurian Britain which orthodox scholarship won't reach for centuries. Edgestow, the tiny, unindustrialized university town, lies in the heart of ancient Logres; Cure Hardy, the quiet, backward, enchanting agricultural village, has preserved the name of Ozana le Coeur Hardi, an Arthurian knight. The historical Merlin lies asleep under Bragdon Wood. And Ransom, who appears to us as a simple "sedentary" scholar in the first two books, suddenly emerges as the awesome Pendragon of Logres and the Fisher-King. Lewis thus uses only a few parts of the Arthurian legend in his own myth. The background of these ideas is as follows:

The Arthurian legend itself perhaps originates as far back as the Welsh *Mabinogion*, which simply mentions in passing a man who goes to someone named Arthur for help. A sixth-century priest named Gildas states that the Britons fought under an Ambrosius Aurelianus at the siege of Badon Hill. In 800, Nennius fills in the details of this battle in his book *History of the Britons;* he says "magnanimous Arthur," twelve times chosen commander, the kings, and the military force of Britain fought against the Saxons. In the twelfth battle, "a most severe contest," Arthur single-handedly killed 940 men at the hill of Badon!

So Arthur was probably a real sixth-century war-leader, minor noble, or chief who won the battle of Badon Hill, a king of ancient Britain, and a conqueror of many countries. But his history soon became embellished throughout the centuries as various authors slowly sprinkled in so many fanciful tales of love affairs, magic, miracles, and monsters that

Arthur emerged as a national and almost unbelievable hero. One such writer was Geoffrey of Monmouth, who describes Arthur in his work *History of the Kings of England* (1150). The usual source, however, is Sir Thomas Malory's *Morte d'Arthur* (1470, 1485). Through oral storytelling and the additions of writers such as these, the history of Arthur developed into a legend, including details of the Round Table, the various knights (Galahad, Percival, Gawain, Lancelot, Tristan, and the others), and the story of the Holy Grail (cup used by Christ at the Last Supper, having supernatural powers). The legend became a substantial part of English tradition, and so adds greater magnitude to the simple story of St. Anne's vs. Belbury.

Logres

Dimble relates Malory's version of the Arthurian legend in which he compares three groups of people: those in the center, such as Guinevere and Lancelot, who are courtly and not particularly British; the "dark people," such as Morgan le Fay and Morgawse, who are very British, hostile, and mixed up with magic; and Merlin, who is British and not hostile. This is the same division of forces into which St. Anne's and Belbury divide themselves: Logres and Britain, with Merlin as "agent."

Logres comes from the Welsh "Lloegr," both a fairyland within Britain, or another name for Britain itself. The term was possibly first used as a name for Arthur's land in Chretién of Troyes' story *Lancelot.* Lewis's source, however, is probably Charles Williams, whose Logres represents God's rule on earth, a perfect union between Heaven and earth. Taliessin must prepare a chaotic Logres for the coming of the Grail. Logres represents a perfect order and religious civilization, a human political body in harmony with God's spiritual law and will. Grace Ironwood says there is an order of law which is divine and transcends human affairs.

Britain is the opposite of Logres, representing the secular will of man, apostasy, and chaos: "Something we may call Britain is always haunted by something we may call Logres. Haven't you noticed that we are two countries? After every Arthur, a Mordred; behind every Milton, a Cromwell." England is the swaying to and fro between Logres and Britain.

The group at St. Anne's, called a "company," was chosen by Maleldil and is all that remains of Logres in Britain—"the remnant." Logres has existed throughout history to keep England from becoming Britain. But Logres is part of a small group; Lewis says only one-tenth of the population are Christians. According to Dimble, there was a moment in the sixth century when Logres almost succeeded in breaking through and we discovered the "haunting." But it has never totally succeeded in the past. That is why the events of *That Hideous Strength* are said to affect the whole future of England. At the end of the story, while Britain has lost the battle it will rise again and there will be "other Edgestows." Just as Logres is England's "haunting," each country has its own "Logres," and the healing of the entire earth depends "on nursing that little spark, on incarnating that ghost, which is still alive in every real people, and different in each." Earth will not be whole until Logres dominates Britain, the "haunting" of every other country is also in control, and Reason, "divine clearness," "the order of Heaven," is truly enthroned everywhere. So the battle is larger than a simple conflict with the N.I.C.E., or even Logres vs. Britain, or the Logres of a particular country vs. its evil. It involves a warfare between order and chaos, good vs. evil eldils, that reaches to the heavens themselves.

The contrast between Logres and Britain can be seen in the differences between the lifestyles and organization of St. Anne's and Belbury. St. Anne's has a definable hierarchy—it is an organization controlled by Maleldil and headed by Ransom; yet all members are still *spiritual* equals. They do not choose to join, but are rather "called" by Maleldil into a company enjoying great companionship and trust. Theirs is a world of openness, conversation, sensitive relationships. Belbury, on the other hand, which is really run by the Bent Oyarsa and his evil eldils (Macrobes), has no apparent organization and is, in fact, chaotic. Apparently, Wither *intentionally* directs things that way because it "works"! No one seems to know who to report to; all is characterized by vagueness, uncertainty, secret parleys, bickering, behind-the-back whispers, and distrust, with everyone trying to penetrate some Inner Ring. All is artificiality, with no communication. One is "drawn in" to N.I.C.E., for their ideal is the creation of a "single personality" with One Mind and a common cause. St. Anne's has a joyful menagerie of animals—a live-in bear, jackdaw, cat, and so on—free to roam through house and garden. They share a special relationship to Ransom, who has learned on Perelandra man's true kinship with beasts. But at Belbury the rule is vivisection on confined animals.

It is also interesting to note the contrasts between the names of those on the two sides of the battle. The names of those at Belbury suggest barrenness, coldness, sterility, and lack of life, or are at least in some sense derogatory: Blizzard, Feverstone, Frost, Wither, Hardcastle, Steele, etc. On the other hand, the good people in *That Hideous Strength* tend to have ancient or common English names, names that sound like the kind of people one would trust: Arthur and Camilla Denniston, Ivy Maggs, Cecil and Margaret Dimble, etc.

The "company" is an unusual and unlikely crew headquartered in the rambling old house with enchanting garden at St. Anne's. Under Ransom are Arthur and Camilla Denniston, Cecil and Margaret Dimble, Ivy Maggs, Grace Ironwood, Andrew MacPhee, and Jane—a simple young couple, an old professor and his wife, a maid, a stern doctor, a skeptic, and a graduate student! Andrew MacPhee has an especially important place among them, says Ransom, because of his search for truth and facts. A perpetual relaxed humor is found in the exchanges between Ransom and the others, including the huge brown bear, Bultitude. Men and women share all the tasks, but each group has to take separate days in the kitchen so they don't quarrel or get in each other's way!

It may seem surprising that the actual "warfare" waged on N.I.C.E. is accomplished by the evil eldils on their own people, with Merlin as the "trigger." For the "company" Ransom formed was supposed to help fight the danger hanging over England. Yet Denniston, Dimble (who knows Old Solar), and Jane (the seer) search hard for Merlin, but fail to find him. Ransom discusses with Merlin his task, but participates little in the final action. MacPhee complains that the story of Britain's defeat would not even need to mention them: "I'd be greatly obliged if any one would tell me what we *have* done— always apart from feeding the pigs and raising some very decent vegetables."

" 'You have done what was required of you,' said the Director. 'You have obeyed and waited.' " Now they are to prepare for more work because Britain will rise again. However, they must obey a new "head," the Pendragon to be announced the day after their celebration dinner, for Ransom is returning to Perelandra to be cured of his wounds.

The Pendragon and Fisher-King

There "has been a secret Logres in the very heart of Britain all these years, an unbroken succession of Pendragons." Ransom is the present Pendragon of Logres. The Pendragon is the British or Welsh King of Britain (and ruler of the ideal kingdom), descendant of King Arthur. *Pendragon* is the British or Welsh word meaning "dragonhead," because the king had a dragonhead standard. The Pendragons of England are said to give the "push" or "pull" to prod England out of the final outrage into which Britain has tempted her.

Uther Pendragon was King Arthur's father. Arthur, says Dimble, was a man of the old British line, but a Christian and trained general with Roman technique who tried to pull society together and almost succeeded. According to tradition, Arthur did not die but was transported to Avalon, the "Isle of Appels" and a sort of other-world, to be cured of his wounds. He supposedly stands in perpetual guard over England, ready to return as savior; thus, there is a hope that some day Logres will triumph over Britain. Similarly, Ransom does not die or age after his voyage to Perelandra and will return there to Abhalljin (*abhal* means apple in Irish), a cup-shaped land beyond the seas of Lur, to be cured of the wound in his heel.

Lewis says there was an unbroken succession of Pendragons from Arthur on, related to the Plantagenets, and the title was handed down from generation to generation. Fourteen members of the Plantagenets, a royal English family, ruled England from 1154 to 1485. Henry II is considered to be connected with Arthur because during his reign the Abbot of the monastery at Glastonbury, which was identified with Avalon, made excavations to search for Arthur's body.

Lewis says the line went from Arthur to Uther (his brother) to Cassibelaun (king mentioned by Geoffrey of Monmouth). The seventy-eighth Pendragon was an old man dying in Cumberland who summoned Ransom to his bedside and gave him the office and blessing. Ransom is the seventy-ninth Pendragon and will pass on the title before he returns to Perelandra just as *That Hideous Strength* ends. We are told that the future Pendragon would have been Jane and Mark Studdock's child—even Frost notes that they are "eugenically interesting"—but it is now too late for them to conceive. The eightieth Pendragon will no doubt be Arthur Denniston, not only because of his significant first name, but because his wife Camilla is told she carries the "future of Logres" in her body.

Ransom's other name is the Fisher-King, which Lewis says is the name bequeathed to him by his sister in India after she died. It seems his sister was the friend of a Sura in India who told her a great danger was hanging over the human race. So she left Ransom a fortune on the condition that he take her name, and told him a company would form around him. But the name Fisher-King also comes from mythology and is associated with King Arthur through the legend of the Holy Grail. In recent literature the myth is found in T. S. Eliot's famous poem *The Wasteland.*

After Christ's crucifixion, Joseph of Arimathea is said

to have received from Pilate the cup used by Christ at the Last Supper and to have used it to catch some of his blood. This "Grail" was passed onto Bron, Joseph's brother-in-law, whose title was Rich Fisher. The Grail became part of the Arthurian legend and gave it religious significance, his knights going on many a quest for the Grail.

Although the idea of a Fisher-King is traceable all the way back to Welsh myth, the twelfth-century poet Chretien of Troyes is one of the first to tell the adventures of Percival, one of Arthur's knights. Percival one day is directed by two fishermen to a castle. In a great hall he finds an old man, the King of the Castle, sleeping on a couch. He has been wounded in the thigh by the spear that pierced Christ's side. He turns out to be Percival's uncle, of the seed of Joseph, and one of the fishermen who directed Percival, for fishing is the only sport he can participate in. Eventually, the legend developed that this Fisher-King was keeper of the Holy Grail and master of the knights. The name also has connections with the Christian fish (*Ichthys*) anagram that became a symbol for Christ and his followers as "fishers of men." The wound in the thigh was symbolic of the fall.

The similarities to Ransom are obvious. Traditionally, the Fisher-King is King or lord of the land and received a thigh or foot wound. Called the "dolorous blow," this wound was, according to some accounts, inflicted by Balin the Savage; it was considered by others to be either accidental or the result of some sin. The King cannot rise from his couch, but lives in an isolated room of a castle subsisting on the Sacred Host brought to him in the Grail by a woman. Because of this "curse" on the King, the land has become a desolate wasteland; but with his restoration it will be restored as well.

Jane finds Ransom also reclining on a sofa and living solely on bread and wine brought to him by Mrs. Maggs. The bleeding wound in his heel was acquired from the bite of the Un-man sometime during their battle on Perelandra. Believing it is his business to "bear the pain till the end," Ransom refuses painkillers, but will be healed when he returns to Perelandra.

The "wound," of course, has other associations. First, as a "Christ-figure," Ransom is wounded trying to "save" the Green Lady; thus, the injury may be a "symbol" of Christ's wounds in ransoming man from sin. Second, it is the "inconsolable wound with which man is born" as a result of sin. In Genesis 3:15, as we shall discuss more fully later, Satan (the Serpent) is told that Eve and her seed (Christ) would bruise his head (defeat of Satan and victory over sin), while he would bruise her seed's heel (crucifixion). Similarly, the Un-man, the Bent Oyarsa's (Satan's) representative on Perelandra, bites Ransom's heel. But Ransom smashes him in the face before he casts him into the subterranean fire. In *That Hideous Strength,* the "Head" of N.I.C.E. also mysteriously disappears during the destruction of Belbury. Finally, we are reminded of the vulnerable heel of Achilles in mythology, created when his mother tried to make him invulnerable by bathing him as a child in the river Styx. But she held him by the heel and thus left the way open for his death—another symbol of man's mortality.

Merlin

Merlin is one of the most memorable figures from the Arthurian legend. Lewis calls him Merlin Ambrosius, a Christian man and penitent. He said that since no one really knows much about him, an author has a free hand in portraying him.

Merlin comes partly from Nennius' account of a boy named Ambrosius who was both a seer and prophet. But he is essentially a creation of Geoffrey of Monmouth who built upon a prophet named Myrddin from obscure Welsh poems. The most common portrait of Merlin that has survived in legend is that he is a wizard, Arthur's teacher, a prophet, and had a strange birth and end. For example, the writer Robert de Borron supposedly added into the legend the account of Merlin's birth. Trying to imitate the incarnation, a devil found a girl who had made one slip—forgotten to say her prayers—but who discovered her mistake and asked the Church to intercede for her. Thus she gave birth to Merlin instead of a demon, who inherited his father's knowledge and power but not his malice. Other stories say Merlin is the child of a Welsh princess and a demon; some say Nimue, a fairy, and Satan. But Dimble brings up the point that Merlin's father need not have been bad.

According to some versions, Merlin was charmed into a permanent state of enchantment by his mother. One story says Merlin taught a girl named Viviane or Niniane a spell which could leave him enchanted; later she tried it out, casting him into a sleep in Broceliande forest.

At any rate, Lewis takes elements from this background and creates his own character. Dimble says Merlin is an odd creation—not evil but a magician; a fifth-century Druid and member of an ancient Celtic religious order who knows about the Grail. Monstrously tall and very fat, almost a giant, with a red-gray beard and hair, he is like something that ought not to be indoors—a "sense of mould, gravel, wet leaves, weedy water hung about him." As you might expect, Merlin has "culture shock," having been suddenly thrust into an environment 1,500 years later than his own. He is perplexed by the running of Ransom's household, the government, and the customs of everyday twentieth-century life. For fifteen centuries he laid in a "sleep" under Bragdon Wood and is reawakened into our century so that his soul can be saved and his mind "invaded" and used by the Oyeresu, who descend to give him powers. We do not learn exactly what happens to him when he is "used up" after his task is completed, but Jane has a vision of lights and colors running up and down him.

Merlin used magic before it became "black," when the relationship between mind and matter was different than now. So he is a perfect person to be an agent of the Oyeresu, because they want a man pure of heart who also understands both the good and evil use of magic. He represents "the last trace of something the later tradition has quite forgotten about—something that became impossible when the only people in touch with the supernatural were either white or black, either priests or sorcerers," the last vestige of something long before the Great Disaster, before primitive druidism succeeded Numinor.

Merlin is a reminder of what we have got to get back to before the healing of earth can take place. Man's lost relationship with Nature and the perversion of his power over it is seen in Belbury. Scientism ("the enemy"), science as it should be, and what Lewis sees as the ideal union of fact and spirit are examined in the next chapter.

CHAPTER 5: MYTH BECAME FACT: SCIENCE AND SPIRIT IN THE TRILOGY

*Though men or angels rule them, the worlds
are for themselves. The waters you have not
floated on, the fruit you have not plucked, the
caves in which you have not descended . . .
do not await your coming to put on perfection,
though they will obey you when you
come. . . . You are not the voice that all
things utter, nor is there eternal silence in the
places where you cannot come.*

Weston's Philosophy

Lewis said he "detested" Devine and Weston! Likewise, his main character, Ransom, supposedly knew Devine back at Wedenshaw school and disliked him then. Now Devine greedily desires riches and "ocean-going yachts, the most expensive women, and a big place on the Riviera." For this reason, Malacandra's Oyarsa diagnoses his condition as "broken," not bent.

The great physicist Weston, however, is only bent.

At least he is interested in a cause outside himself. Since he modifies his philosophy between the trips to Mars and Venus, Weston holds several points of view which Lewis can attack: the interplanetary reach of man to avoid death of the species, evolutionary changes to improve mankind and allow adaptation to different planets, and emergent evolution.

In *Out of the Silent Planet,* Weston believes in the importance of the race (seed) of mankind, not the individual. Since the race should last forever, it must overcome astronomical distances and spread to other worlds whenever one dies, killing other species and hnau when necessary. Ransom labels this idea that all galaxies can sustain life the "sweet poison of the infinite." Weston also does not consider classics, history, and such "trash" education, but rather feels knowledge must be "useful," an end in itself.

As Satan's emissary to Perelandra, Weston decides that man is really nothing, inseparable from Nature. The movement of all life toward the Life-Force is everything. This Life-Force, explains Lewis, is a sort of mindless and tame "God" which is larger and more intelligent than man, a pure Spirit that contains our portrait of both God and the Devil. What we are "reaching for" is God (dynamism); what we "transcend" is the Devil. Weston thus believes in "emergent evolution," the doctrine that the small variations by which life evolved are not by chance, but rather the purposiveness of this Life-Force. Since the nature of the world is to improve, even bad always works for the better. So, says Weston, he once worked for himself, then for science, for humanity, and now the Life-Force.

Lewis says evolutionism or developmentalism, unlike evolution, insists that cosmic improvements have always been the order of things, whereas evolution allows for some degeneration to have occurred. Lewis attacks such "chronological snobbery"—the assumption that what is new and modern is better than what has gone before and is thus out-of-date. Weston, for example, finding Malacandrian life primitive and stone-age compared to earth's, believes man has the *right* to supersede them.

Lewis said he did not really believe that many scientists at the moment hold Weston's philosophy. But he did think a point of view like Weston's is on the way and wanted to show how dreadful the present tendencies might become. While he thought technology *per se* harmless, he considered a race completely devoted to its own technological power and totally indifferent to ethics to be like a cancer in the universe: "I look forward with horror to contact with the other inhabited planets, if there are such. We would only transport to them all of our sin and our acquisitiveness, and establish a new colonialism. I can't bear to think of it." He was certain man would infect space like he has earth, spreading murder, corruption, dust bowls, and slag heaps, mistreating aliens like he has other races here on earth. Why should he act any differently elsewhere?

There would also be a sentimental and aesthetic loss. The "mythic moon," for example, would be taken from us: "No moonlit night will ever be the same to me again if, as I look up at that pale disc, I must think 'Yes: up there to the left is the Russian area, and over there to the right is the American bit.'. . . The immemorial Moon—the Moon of the myths, the poets, the lovers—will have been taken from us forever." But if we on earth were to get right with God, of course, all this would be changed. Once we find ourselves spiritually awakened, says Lewis, we can go to outer space and take *good* things with us.

That Hideous Strength attacks several other complex issues. Lewis himself boiled the plot down to a confilct of grace against Nature and Nature against anti-Nature (modern industrialism, scientism, and totalitarian policies). In the Preface to the book, Lewis says he chiefly presents ideas found in his slim volume *The Abolition of Man*, which has since been included as one of the Great Books of the World.

The Abolition of Man

Lewis begins *The Abolition of Man* by attacking modern education, one of the many themes of *That Hideous Strength*. Lewis claims he chose the university as a background for the book because it was the only profession he knew, being a college professor himself. Yet he manages to depict the politicking and manipulating within college circles at the sacrifice of pure research as he relates the story of Curry, Busby, and the Bracton fellows at the fringe of the main plot. Mark Studdock is said to have had a "modern education," which Lewis says simply means he was good in subjects that require no exact knowledge.

In *The Abolition of Man*, Lewis says modern education has certain tendencies. Primarily, it tries to teach that value statements are merely statements about the emotions, and emotions, because they are aroused by associations contrary to reason, are contemptible. Frost, for example, argues that all motivations, actions, and feelings are biochemically induced. But Lewis argues that in every culture there is a "Tao"—natural law, traditional morality, a set of objective values—which sets up an objective basis for all values and judgments. In other words, the world has a built-in moral "yardstick."

The "debunking" of emotions through propagandistic techniques is therefore wrong. Lewis illustrates the inconsistency of those who claim to debunk value statements. They try, for example, to derive a system of value from the platitudes of practical reason or by appealing to factual propositions, such as saying preservation of the species is an "instinct." Since these are not the basis for any system of values, says Lewis, they are doomed. Furthermore, if we do not accept the Tao, the moral order of the universe, we will move steadily toward our own constructs built on *man's* assumptions, with a resulting loss of objectivity; for without a belief in some external standard of value, man will be forced to turn to private constructs.

Pictured well by Belbury are some other modern trends. Applied science claims that man will conquer Nature (this is defined as "progress") through eugenics, prenatal conditioning, education, and propaganda based on applied psychological conditioning. Eugenics will allow only demigods to be born: "Man has ascended his throne. Man has become God." But, says Lewis, the result is really the power of some men over others with Nature as the instrument. Furthermore, objects are stripped of their qualitative properties and reduced to "mere" quantity in order to "conquer" Nature, just as mankind itself is treated as a specimen. Ironically, Lewis warns, man will eventually surrender himself to Nature because if Nature is conquered with the Tao, it will essentially have conquered man. Science should, therefore, take care not to "explain away" Nature or "see through" it, be free with the words "only" and "merely," or forget the "whole" in lieu of the "parts."

The N.I.C.E.

Many people believe, as a result, that Lewis is attacking science in his books. But Lewis says he was criticizing not scientists, but what is "growing in the real world as a kind of political conspiracy using science as its pretext." This belief he calls *scientism,* the idea that science or technological process can solve all men's problems, create a paradise on earth here and now, and make us happy, with no connection to inquiry into matter or physical energy.

Lewis considered the only *real* scientist at N.I.C.E. to be Hingest who, of course, is murdered. The next best is Filostrato, but he is not inside the true "circle." N.I.C.E. stands for the National Institute of Co-ordinated Experiments and is "the first attempt to take applied science seriously from the national point of view." As a fusion of state and laboratory, it is free from red tape and economic restraint, and it is internationally approved by such countries as the U. S. and Russia.

Organizationally, N.I.C.E. consists of fifteen department directors with annual salaries of $15,000 per year each (remember, this was in the 1940s); a permanent staff of architects, surveyors, and engineers; its own legal staff and police; twenty pragmatometer operators; and forty interlocking committees. It even has its own special kind of sanitation!

Ironically, however, the organization is nonetheless vague and chaotic. To Mark, Belbury is never really defined; the atmosphere is foggy, warmed, drugged. The Fairy says that is simply how Wither runs the place and it works very well! "When it comes to buildings," says Lewis, "all universities are now N.I.C.E.'s." On the twenty acres which Belbury owns sprawls a hideous Edwardian mansion modeled after Versailles, with cement buildings sprouting on the sides and comparable to an "abortive American hotel and glorified gas works."

N.I.C.E. represents everything Lewis warns about in *The Abolition of Man.* All its goals and actions are in the name of progress; yet it is the enemy of humanity, taking the cover of science being applied to social problems. What is worse, it is interested in harnessing spiritual and magical power, for there is black eldilic energy behind the movement. Belbury thus tries on one hand to see Nature as a machine to be taken to bits, and on the other to use spirits to communicate with her. However, Lewis later admitted he didn't think people in "contemporary rackets" were *really* dabbling in magic.

One of N.I.C.E.'s major goals is to control man's destiny by preserving the human race through selective breeding, conditioning, and manipulation of the brain. Their dream is man as god, Man Immortal, or perhaps even a man-made being who will finally ascend the throne of the universe. Using Nature as instrument and with total indifference to truth, he will concentrate on having power over other men. Only an intellectual nucleus of the race is to be preserved, for war will be the means of eliminating the "lower population" (Frost predicts sixteen more major wars in the twentieth century).

The Head is the first of these "new men," the product of attempts to keep the brain indefinitely, freed from the body, birth, breeding, and death. Yet it is a disgusting network of lights, bulbs, metal, gurgling tubes, a green face, a head with skull removed and its brains "boiling over," beard, nose, colored glasses, slobbering mouth, and antiseptic smells. Lewis was no doubt basing this horrible portrait on experiments actually being done to keep organs alive. But as we learn later, this Head is not really alive but merely conductor for communication with the Macrobes (evil eldils).

The "Inner Ring" of N.I.C.E. firmly believes there is no rational universe, but that morality is simply a by-product of one's physical and economic situation, emotions, and chemical reactions. Thus, the function of the Objective Room, with its ill proportions, lopsided door, spotted floor and ceiling, and surrealistic pictures, is to replace normal human reactions with total objectivity. Required to perform all sorts of petty obscenities, Mark is encouraged to regard religion as grotesquely evil and insignificant.

Man is to control his environment as well: "Nature is the ladder we have climbed up by, now we kick her away." Filostrato hopes that someday earth will be totally free and clean of all organic life. Aluminum trees on which wind-up birds will perch will replace our lush and fragrant forests; chemical substitutes will replace the atmospheric properties of trees and foods. How delightfully free man will be from birth, breeding, beauty, and death! Filostrato looks to the half of the moon facing earth (the work of the Bent Oyarsa) as his ideal, with its clean purity resulting from a dearth of grass, plant life, and dust.

The garden at Belbury is appropriately neat and trim, designed like a "municipal cemetery" with trees dotted about, winding paths outlined with white pebbles, and immense, shaped flowerbeds. The garden at St. Anne's is, in contrast, "natural," somewhat reminiscent of the enchanting gardens in *Peter Rabbit* or *Alice in Wonderland.* In fact, everyone at St. Anne's is interested in the "natural": MacPhee and Grace work in the garden; the Dimbles' home and garden are famous for their beauty; Ivy and Ransom are good with animals; the Dennistons like "Weather."

N.I.C.E.'s attempts to enslave Nature and exercise power without reverence for life result in a river not unlike many of today that flows opaque and thick with mud and "sailed on by endless fleets of empty tins, sheets of paper, cigarette ends and fragments of wood, sometimes varied by rainbow patches of oil." Lewis appropriately symbolizes N.I.C.E.'s handiwork by the dank, waxy yellow fog that blankets the entire countryside for days on end.

Unlike the freedom and special relationship with the animals of St. Anne's, N.I.C.E. advocates experimentation on live animals—vivisection—which Lewis attacks in *That Hideous Strength,* as well as in a pamphlet written for the National Anti-Vivisection Society of London. Lewis believed that the arguments that man is superior to animals and that such experiments can lead to discoveries that will alleviate his suffering are not grounds for justifying the infliction of pain; they might just as well lead to experiments on human subjects. The Institute nevertheless has "thousands of pounds' worth of live animality" which it "could afford to cut up like paper on the chance of some interesting discovery." How appropriate that Belbury is clawed and bitten to pieces by means of an uprising of its own loosed animals!

N.I.C.E. is likewise kind to criminals with its reformation ("remedial treatment") instead of retributive punishment. For example, Ivy Maggs's husband, a petty thief about to be released from jail, is instead sent to Belbury for this treatment. Lewis believes that such so-called "humanitarian" measures are in reality cruel and unmerciful because they remove the concept of justice (desert) by not giving the criminal a definable punishment for his sin or allowing him his rights. Rather, crime is viewed as a "disease" needing a cure. The criminal, who ceases to be a person, is thus placed in the hands of "experts" and psychotherapists instead of a jury. These "experts" inflict an indefinite sentence on him; their only consideration is deterring others. According to Fairy Hardcastle, "Desert was always finite: you could do so much to the criminal and no more. Remedial treatment, on the other hand, need have no fixed limit; it could go on till it had effected a cure, and those who were carrying it out would decide when *that* was. And if cure were humane and desirable, how much more prevention."

One of N.I.C.E.'s chief means of corruption of what it cannot touch through experimentation or treatment is through propagandistic use of the press. Lewis strongly disliked newspapers and avoided reading them. But N.I.C.E., through Mark's carefully planned and written articles, lies to the public to plant the attitudes it wants in Edgestow. Whereas the educated class will believe anything, says Fairy, the workman, who enjoys reading football results and human interest or gore stories, has to be "reconditioned."

Because of his many criticisms of Belburian philosophies and scientism, Lewis has been accused of attacking science. But it should be emphasized that Lewis described himself as a rationalist: "though I could never have been a scientist, I had scientific as well as imaginative impulses, and I loved ratiocination." His writings show his awareness of the limits of science, its methodology, and its rightful status as a mode of knowledge. His views are shared by many scientists and philosophers of science.

Part of the confusion arises because science has become associated with a method that deals with fact—what can be observed by careful, controlled experiment. This type of science developed primarily in the seventeenth century, when collection of data, measurement, and repeated experimentation gained prominence. Even until the nineteenth century, science was equated with exactitude, precise measurement, objectivity, controlled observation, and verification. As a result, it is popularly believed that science puts us in touch with reality, while other types of thought, such as moral or metaphysical, do not; they merely describe our subjective feelings, as Frost believes.

Like twentieth-century scientists themselves, Lewis insisted that this view of science is narrow and inadequate; so he sought to redefine the role of science and its correct place in society. He defined science simply as a concern with "finding things out," an escape from "belief and unbelief into knowledge." Experiments allow us to watch how things behave in order to predict and eliminate the peculiar and unique. Grace

Ironwood, however, points out that these supposed unbreak-able laws of the universe, the little regularities we have observed on earth for a few hundred years, "are only the remote results which the true laws bring about more often than not; as a kind of accident." Popular notions of science also mislead by believing that only the empirically observed is ultimate reality, whereas the trilogy makes it clear that there is an even larger, unseen world *full* of creatures who wage an invisible warfare with man's destiny at stake.

Lewis feels that our misconceptions about science, past cultures, other creatures, Nature need drastic revision. We have lost sight of the individual object and person in our eagerness to advance our lifestyle. What we need, he says, is "recovery," a new way of seeing things.

Recovery

Lewis agrees with Tolkien's assertions in "On Fairy Stories" that fantasy can give us the sense of wonder, a cleansed vision of the world, thus strengthening our relish for real life. Like Ransom returning from Malacandra eager to drink in the air and rain with every pore, embracing each smell and even blessing the mud, we too can look at the "real world" with renewed awe, pleasure, and bewilderment. The boy "does not despise real woods because he has read of en-chanted woods," writes Lewis; rather, "the reading makes all real woods a little enchanted." Things hidden by the "veil of familiarity" have rich significance restored to them. As re-corded in the final chapter of *Out of the Silent Planet*, Lewis and Ransom decide that if they can just change their readers' conception of space to that of "heaven," their book will be worthwhile. Most readers of the trilogy would no doubt agree that the books turn "inside-out" many of our views of things: space is *full*, not empty; our egotistical conceptions of other creatures, our own planet, even of man himself are wrong.

The tendency of our age, however, has been a dimin-ishing concern for objects and an increasing compulsion to dissect them. Ingrained in each of us is the idea that we arrive at the reality of something and, in fact, "possess" it by analysis. In the Middle Ages, on the other hand, men like Merlin were part of an old order in which matter and spirit were one, every operation on Nature a personal contact which involved loving, reverencing, and knowing the spiritual qualities of Nature. Even metal could not be used on plants. Every operation on Nature was "a kind of personal contact, like coaxing a child or stroking one's horse." According to Lewis, there were also neutral intelligences in earth which were neither good or bad and whom men could encounter in their investigation of plants and minerals. Man was more in touch with these powers and spirits behind Nature, as well as the secrets, myths, and mysteries locked within it.

Now, says Lewis, the universe is divided into two halves—the natural and supernatural—and we are encouraged never to think of both in the same context. The "new astronomy" beginning in the seventeenth century reduced Nature to the mechanical instead of the genial and animistic. After medieval man "came the modern man to whom Nature is something dead—a machine to be worked, and taken to bits." The world was thus emptied of its indwelling spirits, as well as the old mythical imagination through which man could identify with Nature and see the sun as a god rather than a collection of gases. "The soul has gone out of the wood and water," Ransom laments. As Lewis illustrates so well in his books (for example, *Prince Caspian*) Nature has, in effect, "hidden" herself from us because man has maltreated and manipulated her.

In *The Abolition of Man*, Lewis points out that in order to understand Nature, we have reduced it to a category or an abstraction and thus lost sight of its individuality and divinity. Mark Studdock's education, for example, "had the curious effect of making things that he read and wrote more real to him than things he saw. Statistics about agricultural labourers were the substance; any real ditcher, ploughman, or farmer's boy was the shadow. Though he had never noticed it himself, he had a great reluctance, in his work, ever to use such words as 'man' or 'woman.' He preferred to write about

'vocational groups,' 'elements,' 'classes,' and 'populations.' "
But Ransom realizes that "Nothing was more or less important than anything else, nothing was a copy or model of anything else."

There are thus two ways of looking at things: one is
to see *through* them as instances of a general species or
phenomenon; the other is to see them both *as they are* in
themselves and, more importantly, *along* them to the Source
to whom they point. Ransom has to go to another planet in
order to simply realize that Nature herself is a thing in her
own right, separate from us and important for her own sake.
Describing his entire encounter as "too definite for language,"
Ransom sees life on Perelandra as a "colored shape." He had
once thought of space as a "black, cold vacuity, the utter
deadness, which was supposed to separate the worlds." Yet,
"pulsing with brightness as with some unbearable pain or pleasure, clustered in pathless and countless multitudes, dream-
like in clarity, blazing in perfect blackness, the stars seized all
his attention, troubled him, excited him." The name *space*
becomes a "blasphemous libel" for such an "empyrean ocean
of radiance." How can one call it dead when he feels life pouring into him every minute?

To Ransom's surprise, space is *full,* an excess vitality
of life, the womb of living creatures where heat and light take
on new qualities. He even has to believe in the old astrology
as he feels " 'sweet influence' pouring or even stabbing into
his surrendered body. . . . He felt his body and mind daily
rubbed and scoured and filled with new vitality." Earth, as we
think, is not a ball spinning through empty space, but in a
"densely inhabited and intricately structured medium." This
heaven is "tingling with a fulness of life for which infinity itself
was not one cubic inch too large." Constantly does Ransom
feel a sort of "lift and lightening" of the heart, a "soaring
solemnity," a "sense, at once sober and ecstatic, of life and
power offered in unasked and unmeasured abundance."

Whereas Ransom had also once thought of other
planets as rocky desolations, Malacandra and Perelandra, he

learns, are extraordinarily beautiful. But in contrast to the fullness and vitality of space itself, the planets seem to him, as they are to the eldila, mere holes or gaps in the living heaven. The Green Lady calls them "little lumps of the low swimming in the high." Moreover, earth itself becomes in this perspective a mere dead, silent, cloudlike waste-space. Ransom's peek at earth from the sorn's telescope is "the bleakest moments in all his travels."

Similarly, Ransom had thought of other creatures as the traditional horrible, monstrous, abominable science fiction bogies with feelers, tentacles, horns, stings, jaws, and bulbous eyes. But he learns that there are two ways of viewing everything, depending upon "where you are standing" and how much you know about it. For example, if you looked at a hross from an earthly perspective, it became abominable and disgusting—"a man seven feet high with snaky body, covered, face and all, with thick black hair, and whiskered like a cat." But from another perspective it became delightful, with everything an animal ought to have: "glossy coat, liquid eye, sweet breath, and whitest teeth—and added to all these, as though Paradise had never been lost and earliest dreams were true, the charm of speech and reason." Likewise, under the influence of the Director, Jane is suddenly able for the first time to see mice as they really are—"not as creeping things but as dainty quadrupeds" or "tiny kangaroos."

Ransom, in turn, begins to see men from a Malacandrian point of view. The ugly pfifltriggian portrait of him chiseled in stone, he realizes, is an idealization of humanity. With these same eyes is he able to see Weston and Devine coming toward him as figures with thick, sausagelike limbs, pear-shaped bodies, square heads, heavy narrow feet, lumped and puckered faces, and variegated flesh fringed with dark bristly substance before he recognizes them as men.

In "The Ethics of Elfland," G. K. Chesterton suggests that we look at *all* things in a new way. Like Robinson Crusoe, a man on a rock blessed with just a few precious objects, each little object in the world can be viewed as an item saved from a wreck: "The greatest of poems is an inventory. Every kitchen tool becomes an ideal because Crusoe might have dropped it in the sea. It is a good exercise, in empty or ugly hours of the day, to look at anything, the coalscuttle or the bookcase, and think how happy one would be to have brought it out of the sinking ship on to the solitary island."

How renewed and refreshed Jane Studdock is after her visit with the Director! Whatever she sees or thinks of in the train home leads her to joy: "She saw from the windows of the train the outlined beams of sunlight pouring over stubble or burnished woods and felt that they were like the notes of a trumpet. Her eyes rested on the rabbits and cows as they flitted by and she embraced them in her heart with a merry, holiday love. . . . She also rejoiced in the consciousness of her own beauty." The delightful Mr. Bultitude has "no prose" in his life at all. Rather his "cupboard loves," such as the goodness he tasted from a tin of golden syrup or the caress of a warm and loving hand, "were for him quivering and ecstatic aspirations which absorbed his whole being, infinite yearnings, stabbed with the threat of tragedy and shot through with the colours of Paradise." Every single moment of his life is what Lewis would call "mythic."

Myth

Central to Lewis's story is the sad fact that earth is in a "bent" and "silent" state as a result of the fall in Eden. The consequence has been a separation of myth, truth, and fact; body and soul; matter and spirit; God and man. On Perelandra, Ransom recognizes that "the triple distinction of truth from myth and of both from fact was purely terrestrial—was part and parcel of that unhappy division between soul and body which resulted from the Fall." Yet he is also aware that the division happily is neither wholesome nor final because the Incarnation was the beginning of its disappearance. In *Miracles*, Lewis says: "Nature and spirit, matter and mind, fact and myth, the literal and the metaphorical, have to be more and more sharply separated, till at last a purely mathematical universe and a purely subjective mind confront one another across an unbridgeable chasm. But from this descent also, if thought itself is to survive, there must be re-ascent and the Christian conception provides for it. Those who attain the glorious resurrection will see the dry bones clothed again with flesh, the fact and myth re-married, the literal and metaphorical rushing together."

Nowhere is this more vividly seen than in Ransom's extraterrestrial discovery that what had always been "mythology" on earth is real and living in another world: "Our mythology is based on a solider reality than we dream." The small coiled dragon with scales of red gold, for example, suggests to him that things like dragons which have for centuries appeared on earth only as "myth" might be scattered through other worlds as realities. In fact, on Perelandra he feels as if he is really "enacting" a myth. *That Hideous Strength* suggests that once things even on earth were not as "separate" as they are now. Merlin is the "last vestige of an old order in which matter and spirit were, from our modern point of view, confused."

Since the fall in the Garden of Eden, man has separated subject from object, the phenomenal from the invisible numinous world, and *how* he experiences from *what* he experiences. The first result of this split was the demythologization of the physical world, which has taken us further and further away from the meaning of objects. In his Preface to D. E. Harding's *Hierarchy of Heaven and Earth,* Lewis writes: "At the outset [the ancient world view] the universe appears packed with will, intelligence, life, and positive qualities; every tree is a nymph and every planet a god. Man himself is akin to the gods. The advance of knowledge gradually empties this rich and genial universe: first of its gods, then of its colours, smells, sounds, and tastes, finally of solidity itself as solidity is imagined." "Reductionists" like Frost thus see all as "facts," classifying things as either "subjective" or "objective." Consequently, many people believe that only science can put us in touch with reality. Any other type of thought is simply subjective and therefore invalid. The naturalist, Lewis warns, begins to then further strip the universe of its significance by telling us that nothing really exists *behind* Nature either. In this way, our present world has been drained of qualities of the supernatural and the wonderful.

But a worse result is that man himself has been emptied of all meaning: "The masters of the method soon announced that we were just as mistaken . . . when we attributed 'souls' or 'selves' or 'minds' to human organisms, as when we attributed Dryads to the trees. . . . We, who have personified all other things, turn out to be ourselves mere personifications." There is thus a tension between man's ideal nature—somewhat like the Green Lady and King—and his fallen condition.

One of the chief reasons for Lewis's conversion to Christianity was his realization that it is impossible to perceive reality apart from experiencing it: "As thinkers we are cut off from what we think about; as tasting, touching, willing, loving, hating, we do not clearly understand. The more lucidly we think, the more we are cut off: the more deeply we enter into reality, the less we can think." In other words, once we begin to examine our experience of reality, we are cut off from the object and left with only an abstraction, a mental construct. Since man will always be limited in his knowledge because of this gap between experience and perception, he needs both reason and imagination. As J. R. R. Tolkien explains in "On Fairy Stories," the "secondary world" created by the imagination presents the world that lies behind appearances. Since this world, in fact, is even more real than the world of "fact" we see in space and time, *both* worlds are necessary parts of the whole truth.

Now Lewis believed that the only way to unite these two modes of experience is through metaphor, the most perfect form of which he defines as "myth." Despite the conventional ways of using this term, Lewis defines myth in his own way. Myth, says Lewis, conveys realities which cannot be expressed or even known in any other way. Lewis believes man has been cut off from truth because of sin, but he can still get glimpses of it through myth. Reality is much "larger" than the rational or what can be observed through the senses, and myth allows man to rise above these. At the heart of myth, in fact, is actually a revelation of God. Even pagan myths contain truths about God—"gleams of celestial strength and beauty falling on a jungle of filth and imbecility," as Ransom puts it.

In *An Experiment in Criticism,* Lewis gives an example of what he means by myth. He tells the basic plot of the Orpheus and Eurydice story, plus the mere plot summaries of two other stories. While the first makes a powerful impression on most readers, the other two stories are dull and boring. The appeal of the Orpheus story, Lewis explains, is something beyond its embodiment in a literary form, because simply hearing the plot strikes and moves us deeply. This is because the plot "is only really a net whereby to catch something else. The real theme may be, and perhaps usually is, something that has no sequence in it, something other than a process and much more like a state or quality." Thus, we need only hear a brief summary to *feel* the quality inherent in the story; because it is so much "larger" than words, myth allows us to go beyond the limitations of language. "In the enjoyment of a great myth we come nearest to experiencing as a concrete what can otherwise be understood only as an abstraction. At this moment, for example, I am trying to understand something very abstract indeed—the fading, vanishing of tasted reality as we try to grasp it with the discursive reason. . . . But if I remind you, instead, of Orpheus and Eurydice, how he was suffered to lead her by the hand but, when he turned round to look at her, she disappeared, what was merely a principle becomes imaginable."

Lewis goes on to say that since we do not look for an abstract "meaning" in this myth, we may find it surprising that he seems to be doing so. But by tacking on meaning the story becomes not myth, but allegory: "You were not knowing, but tasting; but what you were tasting turns out to be a universal principle. The moment we *state* this principle we are admittedly back in the world of abstraction. It is only while receiving the myth as story that you experience the principle concretely."

.   A myth cannot be an allegory, a story in which characters or events "represent" abstract ideas because, says Lewis, this shows what man already knows. It is also not a parable, legend, or fable. Instead, myth "goes beyond the expression of things we have already felt. It arouses in us sensations we have never had before, never anticipated having, as though we had broken out of our normal mode of consciousness and 'possessed joys not promised to our birth.' It gets under our skin, hits us at a level deeper than our thoughts or even our passions, troubles oldest certainties till all questions are re-opened, and in general shocks us more fully awake than we are for most of our lives."

The recovery of the "mythic" vision involves not only a renewed perspective on Nature and individual objects, but man himself. As we have seen, the medieval world view painted a picture of an intricately structured universe in which man occupied a definite and important link between the angels and animals; the Arthurian legend also showed man to be a key member of a "company" brought together to save earth from impending chaos and danger. In a century when man has lost his selfhood and is described by such metaphors as cockroach, hairy ape, bloodblister, and rat, Lewis has, as we shall see, a refreshing view of the individual with a special role in a divinely patterned universe.

CHAPTER 6: MAN AND HIS WORLD IN THE TRILOGY

Because we are with Him, each of us is at the
centre. . . . When He died in the Wounded
World He died not for men, but for each man.
If each man had been the only man made, He
would have done no less. Each thing, from
the single grain of Dust to the strongest eldil,
is the end and final cause of all creation.

Ransom

Lewis's hero, of course, is Elwin Ransom (not his *real* name) of Leicester, Cambridge, a philologist and fellow of Cambridge College. Like Lewis himself, he is a bachelor, an avid walker and swimmer, a sedentary scholar of languages, an antivivisectionist, has bad eyes and an old war wound, is very charitable, and has a fear of insects! But Lewis says his hero is "to some extent a fancy portrait of a man I know, but not of me." Because he is a philologist, many believe he is based, in part, on J. R. R. Tolkien. Lewis says he made Ransom a philologist chiefly to render his mastery of Old Solar more plausible. His only family is a married sister, Mrs.

Fisher-King, living in India, who later dies and bequeaths to him both her name and fortune.

There is no doubt that Ransom's physical and spiritual change throughout the trilogy is tremendous. When we first meet him reluctantly stumbling into Weston's "headquarters," he is just a tall, round-shouldered man, "about thirty-five to forty years of age, and dressed with that particular kind of shabbiness which marks a member of the intelligentsia on a holiday." Like one of Tolkien's hobbits, he not only doesn't *feel* like any excitement ("the last thing Ransom wanted was an adventure"), but doubts any such thing could happen to him. He also underestimates his courage: "the gap between boyhood's dreams and his actual experience of the War had been startling, and his subsequent view of his own unheroic qualities had perhaps swung too far in the opposite direction." From the very beginning he does seem to be a religious man—at least he says his prayers on Malacandra, pronounces grace over his food on Perelandra, and even proudly tells the Un-man, "You see, I'm a Christian." And yet his transformation spiritually, physically, and emotionally becomes more marked with each stage of his two journeys.

"Something in the air" or society of the hrossa begins to work a change in him. But it is the killing of the hnakra that really makes him feel "grown up" into a new sort of freedom and courage. The sense of duty and responsibility which increases as he goes to the Oyarsa reaches its full strength in his conversation with the eldil and as he translates for Weston. The narrator notes how very much changed Ransom is after his return from Mars.

When he leaves for Perelandra in book two, Ransom is still merely a tall, white, shivering "scarecrow" with gray hairs. As he emerges from the coffin after over one year, though, he is seemingly a new Ransom, ten years younger, muscular, with a pure golden beard, and in such health that he believes Lewis and Humphrey look sick. This time, says Lewis, he has returned even more transformed than he did from Mars.

As we shall discuss in this chapter, it is the struggle

with the Un-man that provides the crisis in which Ransom comes to understand his role and responsibility on Perelandra, and even the very special meaning of his own name. For this reason, many have seen Ransom as a "Christ" symbol. His name, of course, is "Ransom," he suffers from a wound, is apparently in the cave for three days and is "resurrected," and eats only bread and wine afterwards. But Lewis insists that Ransom, like Psyche in *Till We Have Faces,* is only a Christ-*figure* in the sense that every Christian is or should be. While he undergoes a "second infancy" as he is fed by the planet Venus herself after his days in the cavern, his final transformation is brought about by the purifying air of the Holy Mountain. For, we are told, just as those descendants of Adam and Eve lived longer than we do now, so no one who has breathed the air of Venus and the Holy Mountain or has drunk its waters will die easily. Thus, Ransom will never grow a day older, but will be taken back into Deep Heaven to be healed of his wound.

The Ransom of *Out of the Silent Planet* becomes the Director Jane sees before her resting on the sofa, a man of fifty who appears as a boy twenty years old with one bandaged foot: "Of course he was not a boy—how could she have thought so? The fresh skin on his forehead and cheeks and, above all, on his hands, had suggested the idea. But no boy could have so full a beard. And no boy could be so strong. . . . The grip of those hands would be inescapable. . . . This face was of no age at all. . . . For the first time in all those years she tasted the word *King* itself with all linked associations of battle, marriage, priesthood, mercy, and power. . . . The voice also seemed to be like sunlight and gold. . . . Her world was unmade." Now the bridge between the Oyeresu and earth, Ransom is both the Fisher-King (the spiritual leader bruised by evil) and the Pendragon of Logres (political ruler and king). He is Lewis's portrait of what is the true potential of man and his place in God's plan.

Lewis's View of Man

After meeting the Green Lady, Ransom realizes that

the true definition of a human is not a bodily form or rational mind, but the community of blood and experience—and sin—uniting those on earth. The sorns on Malacandra seem impressed by only two things about humans: the amount of exertion required to do things, and the fact that there is just one type of hnau, greatly narrowing our sympathies and thought.

Certainly, in contrast to hrossa, sorns, the Green Lady, and the King, man is pathetically full of fear—predominantly of death, murder, and rebellion. Ransom feels understandably embarrassed before the eldils, and sadly recognizes his pfifltriggian portrait of a "stocklike dummy" with a head sprouting like a fungus as an idealization of humanity. Because of the "dark shadow" which has spread over all earth, man has lost a common language, the sense of time, his longevity, his love of work, and communion with Maleldil. Even worse, he has become a manipulator. The present age, says N.I.C.E., will see the "beginning of Man Immortal and Man Ubiquitous. Man on the throne of the universe." Some one immortal man will become omnipotent: "It is a man—or a being made by man—who will finally ascend the throne of the universe and rule forever."

But there is hope for man, for like the eldils he is a copy of Maleldil himself. Lewis says that because God is the only perfection there is, the King and Queen are only perfect *homo sapiens,* just as eldils are perfect angelic creatures. The Green Lady thus shows what man might have been without the fall in Eden and its resulting sin. Portrayed as a madonna or goddess, she is beautiful, shameless, and young; the calm of her face is unlike any found on earth. To her, growth is measurable in terms of knowledge and experience, not time. She enjoys a wonderful, perpetual communion directly with Maleldil, and yet her purity and peace are unsettled, breakable, and precariously in a state of balance. Since she knows no evil, the following words, as well as all negative words, mean nothing to her: peace, rubbish, my, kindred, home, alone, dead, blood, pain, courageous, fear, keeping, time, property, self, wrong, might be!

Although we see little of her husband the King, Ransom describes his face as being like God but not the same, sculpted with his own hands like a work of art and free of sorrow or wounds. Ransom considers it a terrifying honor to come "at last, after long journeys and ritual preparations and slow ceremonial approaches, into the very presence of the great Father, Priest, and Emperor of the planet Tellus; a thing to be remembered all our lives." Together, the King and Queen appear as "Paradise itself in its two Persons" strolling hand in hand. "I have never before seen a man or a woman," says Ransom in awe.

Lewis admitted it was hard to draw interesting, convincing, good characters like the King and Queen who are better than yourself. To see a person inferior to yourself, all you have to do is to stop doing something such as being vain, greedy, cruel, or envious. But Lewis says to portray a better person involves imagining and prolonging the very best moments you have had. Since we regretfully don't know what it feels like to be good, such characters usually end up like puppets. Thus, Lewis thought it was almost impossible to write about a person like the Green Lady, who had to be both a virgin and a pagan goddess! But if he could only partially succeed, he thought it worth doing, for we have forgotten about man's potential and perhaps see most people as worse than ordinary.

In *The Screwtape Letters,* Screwtape advises Wormwood to "keep pressing home" on his subject the ordinariness of things. Likewise, while Weston claims that he loves mankind in general—the "seed" or "race"—he has no respect for individual "completed" creatures, for "Man is himself nothing." N.I.C.E., in fact, wants an interpenetration of personalities such as to transcend individuality. So as Frost and Wither talk over the possibility of "assimilating" Mark, a copy of *Who's Who* appropriately crashes off the table.

But Lewis warns against the words "mere" and "only" when applied to people, as well as objects or Nature: "There are no *ordinary* people. You have never talked to a mere mortal." Rather, "There is a dignity and poignancy in the bare fact that a thing exists." Screwtape even has to admit that what God wants is for "each man, in the long run, to be able to recognize all creatures (even himself) as glorious and excellent things." Maleldil, we are told, makes no two blades of grass, angels, saints, or nations the same.

In religious and mythological tradition, the significance and separateness of an individual or object is signified by its name. A name is also the incarnation of a being by God's word, thus affirming his identity and allowing him to know "who he is" and thus his true essence. During his tormenting debate in deciding how to fight the Un-man, for example, Ransom hears a Voice declare, "It is not for nothing that you are named Ransom." Then it dawns on him that his name was no accident, but designed along with the pattern of the whole universe. Ransom, in fact, "stands for" Maleldil on Perelandra: "my name also is Ransom."

The sovereignty of God is one of the major themes of the trilogy. Even from the very beginning of his adventure, Ransom's footsteps are being guided. His inability to get lodging, his encounter with Harry's frantic mother, the decision against his better judgment to trek onward to The Rise, even his love of walking and philology—all are divinely guided. He is "called" to Mars. Only later does he learn that eldila protected him all the way to Malacandra and that Oyarsa caused the hnakra to reappear after many years, just so Ransom could escape Weston and Devine. Eldila then help the spaceship back to earth and protect Ransom, despite the fact that the time allotted to make it back has undoubtedly expired. Ransom is then "called" by Maleldil to Perelandra, ever confident in "those who sent him."

As Director at St. Anne's, Ransom declares that *all* works according to Maleldil's divine plan—both he and Merlin, for example, are now "mediums" of his work, just as Weston was the Bent One's medium on Perelandra. " 'I am the Director,' said Ransom smiling. 'Do you think I would claim the authority I do if the relation between us depended either on your choice or mine? You never chose me. I never chose you. Even the great Oyeresu whom I serve never chose me. I came into their worlds by what seemed, at first, a chance; as you came to me—as the very first animals in this house first came to it. You and I have not started or devised this: it has descended on us—sucked us into itself, if you like. It is, no doubt, an organisation: but we are not the organisers.' "

Of course, Ransom had not always believed that everything he became involved in was other than mere chance, and he had always belittled his own importance. But when it is up to him to defeat the Un-man, suddenly he feels all times converging in him; in fact, at that moment he is the "centre" of the whole universe. Until then, the pattern was so large, his earthly perspective so limited, that he just couldn't see it: "The pattern is so large that within the little frame of earthly experience there appear pieces of it between which we can see no connection, and other pieces between which we can. . . . He had been forced out of the frame, caught up into the larger pattern. . . . Before the world was made, all these things had so stood together in eternity that the very significance of this pattern at this point lay in their coming together in just this fashion." He actually becomes eyewitness of this pattern in the form of the Great Dance, where plans without number interlock and loop together in a grand design.

Even the most insignificant particle in the universe has a task or function in the great scheme of things and is not independent of any other: "Love me, my brothers, for I am infinitely necessary to you and for your delight I was made," sing the eldila. The entire healing of earth, says Dimble, "depends on nursing that little spark, in incarnating that ghost, which is still alive in every real people, and different in each." The Un-man tries to persuade Ransom that the earth is stuck in a remote corner of a universe of overwhelming size and vastness with millions of worlds that lead nowhere. As his brain reels at the thought of the true population of the universe, unchronicled eons of time, and the three-dimensional infinitude of space, Ransom begins to fall into the delusion of our century with its concept of great numbers, gases, galaxies, light years, bigness, and loneliness. But a part of him whispers that "the size of a thing is its least important characteristic." This is why the Oyeresu have a law never to speak of size and number to others because they make us pass by what is great and reverence nothings. Similarly, numbers seem to mean nothing to the Green Lady.

Feeling himself frail and unprepared, Ransom is faced nevertheless with the awesome truth that "Either something or nothing must depend on individual choices. And if something, who could set bounds to it? A stone may determine the course of a river. He was the stone at this horrible moment which had become the centre of the whole universe." At this moment of crisis in Perelandra he realizes he is, in fact, the miracle he had been expecting and impatiently awaiting. But he is tempted again and again into thinking, Who cares if two little creatures live or don't live on a particular rock? Why do *I* have to fight? Why was I chosen? What can an inadequate, sedentary scholar with bad eyes and little muscle do, anyway?

Jane Studdock also resists involvement, wanting to live her own compartmentalized little life free of entanglements and interferences. "Why should I be selected for this horrible thing?" she protests. But the answer to that is known only to "much higher" authorities. "You are a more important person than you imagine," Miss Ironwood assures her. So, when the Bible uses "the expression about fighting with principalities and powers and depraved hypersomatic beings at great heights," it means that "quite ordinary people were to do the fighting." Ransom is called upon simply to do his best. But he must *act,* not just believe. That is why Lewis portrays the battle against evil as being a physical struggle, even requiring the shedding of blood. We often do not know until later why we were chosen, says Lewis, but when we do there is no room for vanity because it is never for your chief qualifications!

Although every individual, even an evil one, is part of

a plan and responsible to perform his role accordingly, this is not to say that he does not still have a free will to choose whether or not he will perform his task. Ransom joyously learns that freedom and predestination are really identical. While the Green Lady, for example, believed she was carried totally in Maleldil's will, she really walks *with* it, not even holding his hand. Lewis says that in choosing to follow God's will, paradisal man also gratified his own desire because service to God was his keenest pleasure. "I am his beast and all his biddings are joy," says the Green Lady. So the question, "Am I doing this for God's sake or only because I happen to like it?" did not arise because his desire did not contradict God's will. The Green Lady is, however, in a state of balance, her purity fragile as she treads from "good to good" on her own two feet.

Jane believes religion ought to be a realm where you aren't treated as a thing or possessed, but where your true self is able to expand in freedom, only to find this is exactly what Maleldil allows. Mark, too, of his own will, at last chooses a side—the Normal. For he realizes he alone—not his parents, "the system," or this "age"—is to blame for all his silly choices of the past: "it was he himself—nothing else in the whole universe—that had chosen the dust and broken bottles, the heap of old tin cans, the dry and choking places."

One metaphor which Lewis uses to describe God's use for each of us as free and unique individuals is that we are "a Divine work of art, something that God is making, and therefore something with which He will not be satisfied until it has a certain character." Ransom describes the King as God's "live image, like Him within and without, made by His own bare hands out of the depths of divine artistry, His masterpiece of self-portraiture coming forth from His workshop to delight all worlds." Suppose, Jane thinks to herself, "one were a *thing* after all—a thing designed and invented by Someone Else and valued for qualities quite different from what one had decided to regard as one's true self?" In Maleldil's presence she feels herself a person, "yet also a thing, a made thing, made to please Another and in Him to please all others, a thing being made at this very moment, without its choice, in a shape it had never dreamed up."

But the Un-man twists the use of art by tempting the Green Lady to invent stories or poems about things that "might be," to imagine herself seizing a grand role in the world's drama and placing herself on center stage. Or we can destroy the art of our lives by not accepting our assigned roles or not rejoicing in each moment, or by considering each point of our lives as independent of others. Two people who do not accept their assigned roles are Jane and Mark Studdock.

The Studdocks

Lewis carefully carries the tale of these two lives throughout *That Hideous Strength;* the account of their lost love for each other and their souls' journeys are as carefully paralleled as the stories of St. Anne's and Belbury. Jane wants no part of anything, while Mark yearns to be a part of whatever group is important for the moment.

Twenty-three-year-old Jane Tudor Studdock abandoned her belief in Christianity, along with a belief in fairies and Santa Claus, back in childhood. She attended St. Elizabeth's College in Edgestow and is now working on her doctoral dissertation, ironically about John Donne's vindication of the body. But she has lost her interest in scholarship. Married to Mark for just six months, she already sees marriage as "solitary confinement" and uses her research as an excuse to delay having children. Trying to be a "modern," liberated woman, she scorns femininity, sentimentality, and dainty clothes. Unlike Mark, she avoids being "drawn in" and balks at committing herself or getting "involved."

Mark Gainsby Studdock is a sociologist and graduate of Duke's College in Edgestow and has been a junior fellow of Bracton College for five years. A bit unrefined and clumsy in his treatment of women, a bit bumbling in social graces, he admits his lack of sensitivity to beauty and culture, but likes to be "liked." He does not believe in God and has never believed in Christianity; instead, he is committed to materialism and the Inner Ring.

In *Of Other Worlds,* Lewis says the Inner Ring is one of the major themes of *That Hideous Strength* and one of society's biggest dangers. He defines Inner Rings as informally organized secret societies or cliques which can be found all over society.

Lewis's distaste for Inner Rings can probably be traced back to his own childhood experiences. At Malvern School, he found the students run by a clique called the "bloods"; Mark similarly compares the Progressive Element of Edgestow to "bloods." Then at Magdalen College, where Lewis taught as a don, he found himself dominated by a group of "progressives" led by Harry Weldon (whom many compare to Feverstone), as well as an Inner Ring within the English faculty itself.

Lewis's attitude toward such groups is discussed in his essay "The Inner Ring" published in *The Weight of Glory.* An Inner Ring, he says, has no officers or rules, no formal admission or expulsion; uses slang, nicknames, and allusive conversation; no fixed name except "we"; has no friendship, just desire for power. In an indefinable way, you discover this Ring exists. One moment you are outside it, suddenly inside it the next, all the time unsure who is really "in" and "out." Several concentric rings may exist, such as Frost's program *within* the N.I.C.E. circle.

What Lewis detested about these Rings is that the craving to simply be "inside" and the terror of being left out or being seen with the wrong people may become one of the dominant elements in a man's life. The greatest evil, Mark notes, is the look of fear on an outsider's face. This anguish and longing is the worst thing about the Ring, for it may induce a man like Mark, who is not bad, to do bad things. And as Mark discovers, you shake off or neglect friends whom you really loved and whose friendship may have lasted a lifetime; then, too late, you may find the Ring has lost its appeal.

Mark had been allured from childhood by a society

called "Grip" (an appropriate name!) and the Inner Circle of his twin sister's friends. As a Bracton fellow, he believes the real Ring to be the Progressive Element. But after talking to Feverstone, he realizes there is another Ring to be penetrated and has the "giddy sensation of being suddenly whirled from one plane of secrecy to another." He then progresses to the Inner Ring at Belbury—associated with the library and the company of Filostrato, the Fairy, Straik, Wither, and Feverstone—to the more "Inner" Ring of Frost's program whose center is outside the human race, and even to a very private Ring with the tramp.

The problems of Mark's and Jane's marriage within the planetary story is appropriate. Courtly love was a central theme in Arthurian literature and Charles Williams's poems, both of which Lewis, of course, draws upon in *That Hideous Strength*. The book begins with the word "matrimony" and ends with the reunion of Mark and Jane. While Jane needs humility as a wife, Mark needs to learn how to be a sensitive lover and to set his priorities straight. Jane sees marriage as solitary confinement rather than "mutual society, help, and comfort." While she has to learn that true freedom is found in subjection to her husband and the will of God, Mark discovers his needs by losing his freedom and free will at Belbury. Thus, by taking opposite routes both learn that service and obedience are the necessary ingredients of love.

Lewis's careful unfolding of the story is apparent as we switch back and forth between Jane at St. Anne's and Mark at Belbury throughout the book. This device allows us to see the conflict between Logres and Britain at the individual level. Belbury seeks Mark only in hopes of getting hold of his visionary wife. On the same day, Mark visits Belbury for the first time and returns home jubilant, earnestly hoping to get *in*, while Jane, afraid of her dreams, visits St. Anne's only to return home skeptical and reluctant to become involved. Mark tries futilely to establish the exact nature of his job as Jane is finding out from the Dennistons just how special her dreams are. The fog blankets Edgestow when Mark at last meets the

Head, then begins writing lies for the newspapers; but Jane climbs through the fog into a penetrating clearness and is "unmade" by the Director. Their paths cross over when Mark, becoming afraid and fearing for Jane, visits with Dimble and Jane has a run-in with the Fairy. Now knowing Belbury as the enemy, Mark returns a prisoner, while his wife happily seeks refuge at St. Anne's. Mark secretly plots with the false Merlin; Jane seeks the real one.

Ransom explains to Jane that she has lost love because she has never attempted obedience and humility, which are erotic necessities. Her stumbling block has simply been pride. The Dimbles, the Maggs, and the Dennistons all serve as examples of more or less ideal relationships; for Lewis, believing in hierarchy as a necessity at all levels, saw man as head over wife. Jane confesses that she no longer loves Mark. But Ransom's reply is only that "obedience and rule are more like a dance than a drill—specially between man and woman where the roles are always changing." "Go in obedience and you will find love."

It is as if a change or boundary had been crossed. For in confronting her need to obey, Jane has also come face to face with Maleldil, whose demands begin to press in on her: "She had come into a world, or into a Person, or into the presence of a Person. Something expectant, patient, inexorable met her with no veil or protection between." Feeling her world "unmade" by the Director, Jane lets down all her defenses. For the first time she can truly enjoy the world and her own Self. But her transformation is not cut and dried. Only gradually does she begin to use her gift of vision for Maleldil's work at St. Anne's and thus play her role in the Company.

Whereas she had always thought of religion and spirit as confining and shadowy, her encounter with Maleldil and his people become the largest thing that had ever happened to her. Ironically, she finds herself by losing herself, and with it her pride and unwillingness to obey: "In this height and depth and breadth the little idea of herself which she had hitherto called *me* dropped down and vanished, unfluttering, into bottomless distance. . . . The name *me* was the name of a being whose existence she had never expected, a being that did not yet fully exist but which was demanded." Her discovery is not unlike Lewis's own struggles with conversion described in *Surprised by Joy*.

Mark's journey is very different. Lewis says the various men in Mark appear rapidly until he too "becomes a person" at the conclusion of *That Hideous Strength*. It is not until he is faced with possible death as a prisoner at Belbury that Mark suddenly awakens to the falsity of the Inner Ring. He had always chosen the *wrong* circle, never done what he *really* wanted, never been with people he truly liked, never eaten or drunk what he enjoyed: "The hours that he had spent learning the very slang of each new circle that attracted him, the perpetual assumption of interest in things he found dull and of knowledge he did not possess, the almost heroic sacrifice of nearly every person and thing he really enjoyed, the miserable attempt to pretend that one *could* enjoy Grip, or the Progressive Element, or the N.I.C.E.—all this came over him with a kind of heart-break."

He knows now that if he ever gets free, he will be admitted to the "right" circle only because of Jane. Knowing that she would disapprove of his every move, Mark is always afraid of being himself around his wife. To Mark, Jane seemed "to have in herself deep wells and knee-deep meadows of happiness, rivers of freshness, enchanted gardens of leisure, which he could not enter but could have spoiled." She enjoyed things for their own sake. In fact, it was people like Myrtle in the old days, Pearson, Denniston, and Jane who had always rescued him from the "dry and choking places."

It is not until he is faced with death, the dry and choking truth about the N.I.C.E., the cold Objective Room with its surrealism, the obscenities, the deprecation of religion, that Mark has a clear idea of the Normal and Straight. This he freely chooses. Now he is even able to truly enjoy reading a simple children's story he had begun reading years ago and was ashamed to read at ten.

Lewis tells us little more about Mark and Jane except

that they are now "ready" for each other. It may perhaps seem curious that Lewis ends his trilogy, not with a great battle scene, or with Ransom returning to Perelandra, or with the final victory over Belbury and celebration at St. Anne's, as we might expect. Rather, the story ends peacefully at the quiet lodge, warm and fragrant and bright, situated just past the garden so alive with the touch of the Goddess of Love. Jane thinks first of Maleldil, then of obedience, then of children, of pain, and of death, and at last of Mark and his sufferings. Things are now in their proper order. This, of course, is the sum of earth's story in its present state as first pronounced in the Garden—the pain, the death, but the command to be fruitful and multiply. The healing of earth will only come about when Maleldil sets them right once and for all. We are simply to obey and wait.

CHAPTER 7: MALELDIL AND HIS REIGN: BIBLICAL BACKGROUND AND THEMES

Where Maleldil is, there is the centre. He is
in every place. Not some of Him in one place
and some in another, but in each place the
whole Maleldil, even in the smallness beyond
thought. There is no way out of the centre
save into the Bent Will which casts itself into
the Nowhere. Blessed be He!

Lewis admitted that any amount of theology can be smuggled into a reader's mind "under the cover of romance" without him knowing it. Although he denies that he ever consciously put morals or Christian principles into his creative books, he said that the "imaginative man" in him made him embody his religious belief in symbolical or mythopoeic form, "theologized science fiction." His aim was to strip the Christian message of its "stained-glass and Sunday school" associations and give it a new form. But in a personal letter, Lewis explains outright the "dark secret," as he calls it, to be found in the space trilogy: "You have the angels, the *eldila*. You have Maleldil 'who lives with the Old One'—i.e., God the Father and God the Son. . . . He did and suffered terrible things in retrieving Thulcandra (i.e., was incarnate and crucified in Earth) fighting against the Bent One, the *eldil* who had gone wrong (Satan, the rebel angel). The 'confined and regimented' state of my mind is revealed in the story at every point." Thus, we can see many parallels between Lewis's myth and the biblical account of Lucifer, the fall of man, and God's nature.

Satan, the Bent One, and Un-man

According to the Bible, Satan was once the most brilliant, the most beautiful, the greatest of all the angels, their ruling prince and leader. In Ezekiel 28:11-17, he is described as "full of wisdom, and perfect in beauty"; he was an angel of light (Lucifer means "the shining one"). But he desired to be greater than God: "For thou hast said in thine heart, I will ascend into heaven, I will exalt my throne above the stars of God; I will sit also upon the mount of the congregation, in the sides of the north, I will ascend above the heights of the clouds, I will be like the Most High" (Isaiah 14:13, 14). He then led a rebellion among the angels, and about one-third of them fell with him as God cast him from Heaven. In several places he is called the ruler or prince of this world (John 12:31; 14:30; 16:11), because when Adam and Eve chose to reject God, all animals, man, and earth were transferred to his control. According to the Bible, earth is the scene of an invisible warfare between Satan and God's forces which affects the entire universe: "For we wrestle not against flesh and blood, but against principalities, against powers, against the rulers of the darkness of this world, against spiritual wickedness in high places" (Ephesians 6:12).

But after the fall of man, God also told Satan: "I will put enmity between thee and the woman, and between thy seed and her seed; he shall bruise thy head, and thou shalt bruise his heel" (Genesis 3:15). "Thou shalt bruise his heel" refers to Christ's crucifixion on the cross. "He shall bruise thy head" refers to Christ, born of the seed of woman, who through his resurrection has given a deadly and permanent wound to Satan and so will one day gain final victory over him. In Revelation we are told armies of angels will appear with Jesus at the Battle of Armageddon. At the beginning of the Great Tribulation, a great war will take place in Heaven between Michael, the leader of the holy angels, and Satan (the dragon) with his fallen angels: "the great dragon was cast out, that old serpent, called the Devil and Satan, who deceiveth the whole world; he was cast out into the earth, and his angels were cast out with him" (Revelation 12:9).

At the Second Coming, Satan and his angels will be judged: "And I saw an angel come down from heaven, having the key of the bottomless pit and a great chain in his hand. And he laid hold on the dragon, that old serpent, which is the Devil, and Satan, and bound him a thousand years, and cast him into the bottomless pit, and shut him up, and set a seal upon him, that he should deceive the nations no more" (Revelation 20:1-3). When 1,000 years are up, Satan will be temporarily released. Then, in a final battle, God will cast him and his angels into a lake of fire and brimstone to undergo eternal torment (Matthew 25:41; 2 Peter 2:4; Jude 6; Revelation 20:10).

In Lewis's myth, the Oyarsa of earth was one of the brightest and greatest of Oyeresu who wanted to become like Maleldil and thus rebelled. Desiring to destroy other worlds, he smote the moon and much of Malacandra and now attempts to invade Perelandra. During the Great War, Maleldil drove him out of the heavens, confining him to the earth and region below the moon, where a number of eldila who followed him also reign. Someday the memory of this Black Oyarsa will be blotted out when Maleldil returns to earth in war. Lewis said this Bent One is "Satan, the rebel angel," although only two in sixty reviewers realized he is anyone other than a "mere invention."

Weston becomes the agent of the Bent Oyarsa on

Perelandra because the Bent One is bound to the territory between earth and the moon; thus, Weston helps us see some of Satan's qualities. From the very first time Ransom sets eyes on Weston he detects a "subtly unfamiliar" look in his face, for he is only partially overtaken at first. Soon Ransom can't tell when Weston or the Devil is talking; but unlike the old Weston, he always wears a "devilish" smile and a silly grimace. Whereas Weston was also previously ignorant of Old Solar, the evil eldila have since taught him the language.

Weston appears to become totally overtaken by the Bent One when he calls upon "the Force" to completely fill him. Then, in a spasm that twists his face beyond recognition, his body goes into slavering and chattering convulsions, and he bites clear through a brandy bottle: "The forces which had begun, perhaps years ago, to eat away his humanity had now completed their work. The intoxicated will which had been slowly poisoning the intelligence and the affections had now at last poisoned itself and the whole psychic organism had fallen to pieces. Only a ghost was left—an everlasting unrest, a crumbling, a ruin, an odour of decay."

Thereafter, Ransom describes him as almost a dead man, with expressionless mouth, evil grimace, staring eyes, and heavy and inorganic folds of the cheeks. Here is a whole-hearted evil beyond anything he had ever seen, something one can truly hate. Inside he is merely a black puerility, Nothing: "darkness, worms, heat, pressure, salt, suffocation, stink." Senselessly does he destroy animals and plants with no regard for life. In fact, he has come, says the Un-man, so that the Green Lady might have death in abundance. Unlike the hrossa who welcome death because it leads to Maleldil, Weston remembers his dead grandmother and his bad childhood dreams: "That child knows something about the universe which all science and all religion is trying to hide." His ripping open of the first frog becomes an "intolerable obscenity" because it is the first dead, spoiled thing in that world. This one "struggling little horror" at Ransom's feet becomes a symbol of an awful horror spreading over this perfect planet: "better

. . . for the whole universe never to have existed than for this one thing to have happened."

Evil is depicted in other forms throughout the trilogy. A puzzling presence in Malacandra, for example, is the hnakra, an aquatic monster. Since the name probably comes from the Old Norse *snakr,* meaning snake, the beast seems to be a symbol for evil. Born in the mountains of water in the north, this creature has not been seen for many years, but the Oyarsa calls it to allow Ransom to escape. Apparently, it was originally "let in" to Malacandra under the command of Maleldil and the Oyarsa, representing the cold brought to the planet by earth's Bent Oyarsa.

Yet he is considered both an enemy and beloved of the hrossa; many images of him hang in their houses, for he is the "sign" of all hrossa. They feel his joy, leap with him, know when his roaming time has come; the young even play at being hnéraki. Since only a bent hnau is really evil, they say, the hnakra does not tempt them to evil; but he gives a certain exciting danger to the spirit of the valley. "I do not think the forest would be so bright, nor the water so warm, nor love so sweet, if there were no danger in the lakes," says Hyoi. Thus, this hross feels he "drinks life" because death is in the pool. In other words, because of the possibility of going wrong or of dying, the joy of going right and of living is enhanced.

We are told that earth, however, is under a state of siege and the universe at war, with the two sides ever becoming clearer and clearer: "There is no neutral ground in the universe: every square inch, every split second, is claimed by God and counterclaimed by Satan." This moral conflict is both physical and spiritual. Evil, says Lewis, is merely "spoiled good"; it cannot create, but can "spoil something Another has created. Satan may have corrupted other creatures as well as us." Thus, even scientists at N.I.C.E. were once good, says Ransom. But evil, as Lewis portrays it here and in *The Screwtape Letters,* digests the individual, "melting" him down into Satan. As Frost and Wither themselves are becoming increasingly demon-possessed, Wither says of Mark: "I would welcome an interpenetration of personalities so close, so irrevocable, that it almost transcends the individuality. . . . I would open my arms to receive—to absorb—to assimilate this young man."

In his cell, Mark experiences evil like a "lust," a movement opposite to Nature which spins everything counterclockwise. It has poisoned the entire earth: "However far you went you would find the machines, the crowded cities, the empty thrones, the false writings, the barren beds: men maddened with false promises and soured with true miseries, worshipping the iron works of their own hands, cut off from Earth their mother and from the Father in Heaven. You might go East so far that East became West and you returned to Britain across the great Ocean, but even so you would not have come out anywhere into the light. The shadow of one dark Wing is over all Tellus."

There are two "kinds" of evil, though. One type is ignorance from being "young"—the Green Lady and King, for example, *learn* evil without experiencing it. However, the "darker ignorance" comes from doing it, and its temptations repeatedly arise throughout the trilogy. From the very beginning, false eldila tempt Ransom not to go on to the Rise where Harry is being detained by Weston and Devine. In *Perelandra*, Lewis the narrator begins to suspect Ransom is a mad dupe, even though rationally he knows him to be sane and honest; then he begins to suspect *he* is mad. Evil eldila cause him to forget his pack on the train and want to go back and get it. As he walks on instead, he feels himself drawn "into an interminable argument" as if he were walking against a headwind. Although he wants a barrier or curtain between him and the eldil at Ransom's home, he feels a jealousy and resentment of its attention to Ransom: "Leave you and your familiar alone, you damned magician, and attend to me."

Ransom himself is tempted at every stage of his journey, especially when he evades the idea that he is to *fight* the Un-man. He was prepared for the blasphemy and horror, certainly not the "petty, indefatigable nagging as of a nasty little boy at preparatory school." These two creatures can't be of *that* much importance, he argues to himself. Even his tiny lie to the Green Lady about the scowl on his forehead tears him "like a vomit" and somehow becomes of infinite importance. During his long chase after the Un-man over the water, the dark eldila also tempt him into their way of thinking. He begins to believe in Weston's philosophy that the beauty and inno-cence of this new planet and all the affection he had ever known on earth are but a dream, illusion, "outward show": "What he had called the worlds were but the skins of the worlds: a quarter of a mile beneath the surface, and from thence through thousands of miles of dark and silence and infernal fire, to the very heart of each, Reality lived—the meaningless, the un-made, the omnipotent idiocy to which all spirits were irrelevant and before which all efforts were vain." In the cavern thoughts, fears, and visions of deformed crea-tures fill his brain. "Part of the corruption in us might be the unreasoning horror and disgust we feel at some creatures quite apart from any harm they can do us. (I can't abide a spider myself)," writes Lewis.

Although the Un-man wounds Ransom's heel, Ran-som smashes the Un-man's head, then "in the name of the Father, of the Son, and of the Holy Ghost," hurls him into the subterranean fire.

The Fall in Eden and the Temptation of the Green Lady

Lewis began writing *Perelandra* after completing his *Preface to Paradise Lost,* one of the classic books on Milton's epic poem about the fall of man and the angels. Lewis says the poem got him thinking about what an unfallen Adam and Eve would be like and the purpose of the forbidden fruit.

Although Lewis uses many of Milton's ideas in his own depiction of the temptation, Lewis disliked and aimed to correct in *Perelandra* several aspects of Milton's version. Probably foremost was his distaste for Milton's portrayal of Satan, whom many people find so grandiose and magnificent that they consider him the hero of the poem. Lewis's Un-man is certainly different from the somber and glorious Satan of *Paradise Lost,* as well as our traditional picture of Satan as a gentleman with red cloak and pitchfork. His cruel performer of petty obscenities is merely an imbecile, a monkey, a nasty child who converts Weston to an "it" devoid of personality. In *Preface to Paradise Lost,* Lewis says that drawing a character *worse* than yourself is not difficult.

Lewis also criticized Milton's portrayal of God, whom he felt was too anthropomorphic, cold, merciless, and tyrannical—somewhat like the petty gods of Greek mythology. Milton's depiction of unfallen sexuality was also poor, Lewis thought. Lewis, of course, changed both Milton's and the Bible's accounts by introducing an agent from God—Ransom—who intervenes to prevent Paradise from being lost. The Fixed Land replaces the fruit as the forbidden element. But perhaps Lewis's biggest contribution is his investigation of two important questions: What was the temptation in the Garden of Eden *really* like? What if Eve *hadn't* fallen?

The fall of man is recorded in Genesis 3:1-6—just six verses. Made in the image of God and able to make moral decisions, including the choice to sin, Adam and Eve lived in perpetual fellowship with God. There was but one prohibition: "of the tree of the knowledge of good and evil, thou shalt not eat of it; for in the day that thou eatest thereof thou shalt surely die" (Genesis 2:17). Apparently this was a test to see if they would obey God. Satan is described as taking the form of a shining, beautiful, shrewd, cunning serpent that walked on legs. It was "more subtle than any beast of the field which the Lord God had made."

Satan recalls God's command to Eve: "Yea, hath God said, Ye shall not eat of every tree of the garden?" Planting seeds of doubt, he focuses on the one limitation, implying that God is holding back some good and is thus being unreasonably severe. Eve replies, "We may eat of the fruit of the trees of the garden; but of the fruit of the tree which is in the midst of the garden, God hath said, Ye shall not eat of it, neither shall ye touch it, lest ye die." She omits the words "freely" (they may *freely* eat of the trees in the garden) and "surely" (they will *surely* die if they disobey). Satan picks up on this: "Ye shall not surely die; for God doth know that in the day that ye eat thereof, then your eyes shall be opened, and ye shall be as God, knowing good and evil." Challenging God's word and the certainty of the punishment, Satan leads her to believe God is withholding experiential knowledge of good and evil from them so they will not be like him. But Satan also fails to reveal the *kind* of knowledge they will have if they disobey.

So Eve rejects God's command, believing his motives impure: "When the woman saw that the tree was good for food, and that it was pleasant to the eyes, and a tree to be desired to make one wise, she took of the fruit thereof, and did eat, and gave also unto her husband with her; and he did eat." Adam thus followed, but was not deceived himself (1 Timothy 2:14). The results were physical death, spiritual death (separation from God), and the curse of Adam, including the sorrows and struggles of existence.

First John 2:16 describes the pattern of temptation which Satan uses both here and in his temptation of Christ in the wilderness: "lust of the flesh" (fruit "good for food"), "lust of the eyes" ("pleasant to the eyes"), and "the pride of life" (power to "make one wise").

A major portion of *Perelandra* is devoted to the temptation of the Green Lady. Even though Ransom recognizes that this temptation seems similar to the one which occurred on earth, it is not a mere repetition of it. Rather, there are correspondences among worlds, but no world is like another: "Maleldil never repeated Himself. . . . Nothing was more or less important than anything else, nothing was a copy or model of anything else." These correspondences among planets with similar mythologies allow us to learn the myth of Deep Heaven which, through sin, we have lost.

Lewis here is supposing what the temptation in Genesis *might* have been like, assuming most of the details in the brief biblical account have been left out. Certainly Eve was not an automaton, quick to succumb to the serpent. Rather, the temptation must have been a continual, lengthy process involving subtlety and logic on the part of the Devil. Ransom "did not know whether Eve had resisted at all, or if so, for how long. Still less did he know how the story would have ended if she had." Thus, he intervenes as a participant himself in a new situation. While it seems unfair that it is the Green Lady who has to endure this temptation, the King meanwhile learns "strange things" in Lur about Maleldil, what is happening to the Queen, what happened to Adam and Eve, and of evil, good, anguish, and joy.

The Un-man's temptation strategy really occurs in two stages: the use of logic and argument, then the telling of stories. But perhaps the ground is prepared by Ransom himself. He teaches the Green Lady the difference between earth and Venus, as well as the fact that other creatures have important things to tell her. The Un-man then shows her that she has a self and is a separate being, but needs to become a whole woman. Lewis believes this is the key to the fall of man: putting self first, wanting to be the "centre," and inventing some happiness for yourself outside God. Now that she is "older," argues the Un-man, Maleldil wants her to demonstrate how separate and independent she is by disobeying him. Maleldil sent us up here to tell you this, he claims.

The main part of the temptation hinges on the concept of obedience, one of the main themes of the trilogy. Hyoi, for example, was killed on Malacandra as a result of Ransom's hesitancy to go to Oyarsa immediately rather than hunt. He knows, then, that his order to go to Perelandra for some purpose "comes from much higher up. They all do, you know, in the long run." Now Ransom knows there may be times when we are to obey by taking some great action—such as defeating Satan himself.

The Green Lady is commanded not to sleep on the Fixed Land, but rather on the floating islands. Like the command in Eden not to eat of the tree, the purpose of this restriction is simply so they may be obedient: "only then can we taste the joy of obeying because his bidding is the *only* reason." Good is not the same on all worlds, Lewis suggests. The floating islands thus seem to symbolize God's will and our need to trust in his direction, instead of the security and legality of our own will: "Why should I desire the Fixed except to make *sure*—to be able on one day to command where I should be the next and what should happen to me?" asks the Green Lady. The purpose of the Fixed Land, in fact, is to lead them ultimately to their destined throne as rulers of Perelandra through their obedience and faith. Whereas Ransom finds a paradisal sweetness on the islands, he awakens sore, hungry, and thirsty after his uncomfortable sleep on the Fixed Land and finds the food there austere and prosaic, the beasts less magnificent. Perhaps his nakedness also represents intent to do God's will, the white coffin death to former existence.

Next, the Un-man points out that not only is Maleldil's bidding strange, but unlike any command in our world. Instead, she can think of what *might be,* such as living on the Fixed Land. He says, Maleldil sent us to tell you things like this that you never knew; so if you turn away you are rejecting the fruit given to you. Furthermore, by learning things, you would be becoming older and wiser, as he desires, letting go of Maleldil and Maleldil of you. Certainly, the King would love you more if you knew as much as earth women do. Not only does Maleldil truly long for you to become your own person, but to do otherwise would be to disobey. You see, the purpose of the command is to simply forbid for the sake of forbidding so you can *seem* to disobey and experience full growing-up. Obviously, if it were a good command in itself he would have given it to all worlds. So it is just a test. Earthlings who took a similar test became more beautiful and excelled and, what is more wonderful, allowed Maleldil himself to come to earth as a man. The test is purposely hard, so that only the courageous can experience the "Deep Life."

The next stage of the temptation plays on the idea that it is her duty, planned by Maleldil, to perform some Great

Risk or Deed as a martyr or tragic pioneer, to seize a grand role in a drama. Thus, the Un-man presents tale after tale of noble women who suffered and took great risks for the sake of king and children, but ended up happy and vindicated. Not only would it be cowardice to refuse, but the opportunity might slip; so she must act now or never. Finally the Un-man tries to build up her concept of self by encouraging vanity and egoism by adorning her in the feathered robe, which she admires in his cheap mirror. But mainly he tries to paint her as a great tragic soul. Lewis warns: "Beware of excessive day-dreaming, of seeing yourself in the center of a drama, of self-pity and—of fear." What appeals most to the Green Lady is the idea of benefiting the King by sacrificing herself.

Throughout all his books, including the trilogy, Lewis emphasizes that when a person chooses to fill the center of his life with self, he can only find Hell and nothingness. After all, says Lewis, Hell is just the shutting up of a creature in its own mind. But if God is the center, everything becomes more itself! One reason why earth has no Oyarsa is because everyone wants to be a little Oyarsa. For example, in Lewis's short story "The Shoddy Lands," Peggy's world exists with a swollen image of herself at the center, around which are "grouped clear and distinct images of the things she really cares about."

In contrast, the various "selves" that Jane Studdock encounters during her train ride seem to reflect the various "layers" of herself, with the deepest layer encompassing all of them and being the real Jane. While Jane #1 is girlishly superficial, simply receptive of the Director, recalling his every word and look, Jane #2 tries to control #1 and is disgusted with her. Jane #3 arises from "some unknown region of grace or heredity" and urges her to be nice to Mark. But Jane #4 is a "larger experience," the true Jane who surfaces because of Maleldil's presence with the Director, and who dominates all the others effortlessly in a state of joy "in the sphere of Jove, amid light and music and festal pomp, brimmed with life and radiant in health, jocund and clothed in shining garments."

Lewis also suggests that the root of all evil may be the itch to have things over again, like eating the same fruit, hearing the same symphony twice in one day, or desiring what "might be" or, as Aslan warns in Narnia, what "would-have-happened": "We often, almost sulkily, reject the good that God offers us because, at that moment, we expected some other good. . . . On every level of our life . . . we are always harking back to some occasion which seemed to us to reach perfection, setting that up as a norm, and deprecating all other occasions by comparison. But these other occasions, I now suspect, are often full of their own new blessing, if only we would lay ourselves open to it. God shows us a new facet of the glory, and we refuse to look at it because we're still looking for the old one."

Each moment, each situation, is a gift from God, to be explored for its unique possibilities and potentiality: "every day in a life fills the whole life with expectation and memory"; "the going itself is the path." However, we tend, like Weston, to look always to the future or wake up thinking we own the twenty-four hours of each day. If God controls our routine from minute to minute, then every experience is joy. We should thus prefer the given—this day, this moment, turning from expected to given good instead of making the real fruit insipid by thinking of another. For the fruit you are given to eat, the wave rolled toward you at each moment, is the best of all.

The Bent Oyarsa, however, is said to have clung to the old good for so long that it became evil. We can, in the same way, begin to see things as a means to an end, something to be used for *our* pleasure. Lewis explains that an experience or object becomes a need-pleasure when it gratifies us or we *need* it (e.g., gluttony vs. hunger). In fact, we feel like we are doing Nature a favor simply by pausing to enjoy the fragrance of a garden. The hrossa call this longing with the senses *hluntheline*. But we must be careful not to isolate pleasure in order to have it by itself, without the rest of the experience. Hyoi uses the example of a poem, where the most splendid line becomes "fully splendid only by means of all the lines after it; if you went back to it you would find it less splendid than you thought. You would kill it." Screwtape warns that one of the devils' subtlest modes of attack is warded off by the "man who truly and disinterestedly enjoys any one thing in the world, for its own sake, without caring twopence what other people say about it."

As Hyoi says, a pleasure is only full-grown when remembered. Pleasures of appreciation are the enjoyment of things for their own sakes, the "disinterested" love of the object itself, the feeling "which makes us glad of unspoiled forests that we shall never see; which makes us anxious that the garden or bean-field should continue to exist." The eldila sing that fruit we have not plucked, water we have not floated on, Nature we have not seen do not exist for man or await his coming to be perfect. Thus, Ransom's taste of the waters and fruits of Perelandra is like meeting a new genus of pleasure through all his senses at once.

The Tower of Babel

One of the great symbols for evil and man's pride has been the Tower of Babel, and Lewis draws on this story as related in Genesis 11:1-9. This tower made of bricks in the plain of Chaldea in what was later Babylon was one of the ancient wonders of the world. Its purpose was to make a name for the people by creating a structure which would reach to the heavens and give them great power. At that time, all men spoke one language, just as all creatures in Lewis's myth once spoke Old Solar. But when God saw their vanity, he gave them all different languages and spread them over the earth. This is thus the origin of our word "babble."

The title of *That Hideous Strength* comes from Sir David Lyndsay's description of the Tower in his medieval poem *Ane Dialog (The Monarche):* "The Shadow of that hyddeous strength sax myle [six miles] and more it is of length." According to Lyndsay, Nimrod, a strong hunter of huge stature and bulk, became king, introduced idolatry, and proposed the building of a city and a tower to the stars to dethrone God, a tower five and one-half miles high and ten miles around.

This story is paralleled by the great mansion at Belbury, where the goal is to place "Man Immortal" on the throne of the universe. At the inaugural banquet, first Jules's speech is turned to babble, then Wither's, and finally everyone in the room shouts unintelligible gibberish. "They that have depressed the word of God, from them shall the word of man also be taken away," Merlin explains. Maleldil's wrath is displayed in the earthquakes, floods, and lightning that follow.

But those at St. Anne's experience the presence of Mercury, the god of language himself. Ransom experiences the heart of language and white-hot furnace of speech. They speak puns, paradoxes, fancies, anecdotes, eloquence, melody, "toppling structures of double meaning," "sky rockets of metaphor and allusion." Certainly this scene recalls the coming of Pentecost in Acts 2, when the Holy Ghost descends on the disciples like the rushing of a mighty wind and they speak in various languages.

Maleldil and His Country

In opposition to the Crooked, Lewis presents a clear idea of the Straight. Jane had always thought of religion and the spiritual in a negative sense—a neutral or democratic vacuum where differences disappeared, a gray formalized world of stained-glass attitudes, a "cloud of incense" steaming up from souls to Heaven, "the smell of pews, horrible lithographs of the Savior . . . with the face of a consumptive girl, the embarrassment of confirmation classes, the nervous affability of clergymen." Weston says God is a "spirit." A result of such thinking is that God has eventually become a sort of transcendent and immaterial being, as vague and indefinable as a gas diffused in space.

But Maleldil—Creator of the Universe, Ruler, Lawgiver—actually is "all a burning joy and strength." Lewis describes his presence as a hugeness so intolerably big that Jane feels herself "shrinking, suffocated, emptied of all power and virtue." Ransom, too, experiences him as an unbearable pressure or intolerable weight that crowds the air, making it difficult to breathe. But this effect occurs mainly when he begins to feel independent. If you gave in to it, it became a splendor of "eatable, drinkable gold: which poured into and out of you and made life a vacuum, and gave you a feeling of well being." Jane feels this sense of deep joy as a state of simple honesty and spirituality. The extreme pressure causes such a heaviness in your shoulders and knees that your legs give out and you must sit down or kneel in worship. Like Aslan, Maleldil is also associated with sweet odors.

Jane thus finds an utter contrast between what she had been taught at school to be religion and the "bright, darting, overpowering," the "terror of dreams, rapture of obedience, the tingling of light and sound from under the Director's door, and the great struggle against an imminent danger." For Maleldil is not a tame god, but jealous; he can "unmake" you, because only Maleldil sees a creature as he really is. Like the eldils, Maleldil makes the room seem aslant, because we are out of kilter to God and Heaven. This, Mark learns, is because God is the only objective reference that exists—the "Normal" and "Straight"—which "obviously existed quite independently of himself and had hard rock surfaces which would not give, surfaces he could cling to." The Normal was "solid, massive, with a shape of its own, almost like something you could touch, or eat, or fall in love with. It was all mixed up with Jane and fried eggs and soap and sunlight and rooks cawing at Cure Hardy."

In many of his novels, Lewis almost always associates God and Heaven with the biblical metaphor of light. At the end of *Perelandra,* for example, as all the eldila and creatures gather around the King and Green Lady, Ransom notices that everything is bathed "in a pure daylight that seemed to come from nowhere in particular. He knew ever afterwards what is meant by a light 'resting on' or 'overshadowing' a holy thing, but not emanating from it. . . . The light reached its perfection and settled itself, as it were, like a lord upon his throne or like wine in a bowl, and filled the whole flowery cup of the mountain top, every cranny, with its purity, the holy thing."

As Ransom realizes that the planets are mere holes or gaps in the heavens since space is *full* of life, he considers the possibility that "visible light is also a hole or gap, a mere diminution of something else. Something that is to bright unchanging heaven as heaven is to the dark, heavy earth." For God himself is more perfect light than we know on earth, the "intolerable light of utter actuality."

The Great Dance is described as being woven out of cords or bands of light because each thing, "from the single grain of Dust to the strongest eldil, is the end and the final cause of all creation and the mirror in which the beam of His brightness comes to rest and so returns to Him." Here on earth, however, we are imperfect reflections of God. Ransom sadly notes, "I have lived all my life among shadows and broken images." Lewis uses the limitations of our physical sight to illustrate the limitations of our spiritual vision and different gradations of our spiritual blindness as a result of the fall.

A perfect example is the eldila, whom Ransom finds hard to see because light goes right through them: "The swiftest thing that touches our senses is light. We do not truly see light, we only see slower things by it, so that for us light is on the edge." Just as there are physical realities which we cannot see, so too the impaired nature of our spiritual vision blinds us to spiritual reality. Light is thus an appropriate metaphor for exemplifying that we cannot know the whole of reality or go "behind" events. Light is only a pointer to something else: Concrete Reality, Light Itself, Maleldil. Although we cannot see the source of light, we are nevertheless conscious of it, and it enables us to see things.

We have a longing for beauty because we have a hint of it on earth. Lewis writes, "We do not want merely to *see* beauty. . . . We want something else which can hardly be put into words—to be united with the beauty we see, to pass into it, to receive it into ourselves, to bathe in it, to become part of it." Like our conceptions of God, our dream of "heaven" is also vague and shadowy. The human soul, says Lewis, has a *Sehnsucht,* a crying and longing within our unreal world for a beauty which lies "on the other side of existence." In his books, however, this realm is portrayed as existing not only within the center of each thing that exists, but as a more solid, positive, large, concrete reality than we can imagine. In a way, Weston was right when he said our whole life is an illusion or dream. He claims reality is neither rational nor consistent, that all earth is appearance and that reality lies beneath the surface. In the cavern, Ransom starts to think he is right because any other world seems like an illusion. But he is right only in that life is weak and flimsy to the solid reality it reflects. Thus, Ransom finds his experience on Perelandra too definite for words; he sees reality and thinks it a dream. "You see only an appearance, small one," he is told. "You have never seen more than appearance of anything." While to many people, corporality and locality seem inapplicable to spirit, even eldila are depicted as being so solid that they can pass through a wall as if it were a cloud.

Before he became a Christian, Lewis read Samuel Alexander's book *Space, Time, and Deity,* which discusses the fact that it is impossible to perceive reality apart from experiencing it. As Lewis describes in *Surprised by Joy,* this insight was instrumental in his coming to God. All his life, Lewis had searched for joy. His first experiencing of longing occurred one day as he stood by a flowering currant bush: "It is difficult to find words strong enough for the sensation which came over me. . . . It was a sensation, of course, of desire; but desire for what? . . . It had taken only a moment of time; and in a certain sense everything else that had ever happened to me was insignificant in comparison." But he was later to discover that he had mistaken the objects of joy for joy itself. As he sought for the source of joy, Lewis found he was left with only its tracks.

In "The Weight of Glory," he describes a similar longing of all men for a "far-off country": "it is a desire for something that has never actually appeared in our experience. We cannot hide it because our experience is constantly suggesting it. . . . Beauty, the memory of our own past . . . are not the thing itself; they are only the scent of a flower we have not found, the echo of a tune we have not heard, news from a country we have never yet visited."

Ransom expects that the longing for the floating islands was in him before time itself: "The cord of longing which drew him to the invisible isle seemed to him at that moment to have been fastened long, long before his coming to Perelandra, long before the earliest times that memory could recover in his childhood, before birth, before the birth of man himself, before the origins of time." The forest smells create a new hunger and thirst in his soul. As he witnesses the Great Dance, he is drawn up with "cords of infinite desire" into its stillness, quietness, privacy, and freshness and comes, as it were, "into himself." Similarly, as Mark heads toward St. Anne's, he experiences health, youth, pleasure, and longing blowing toward him. As in all Lewis's books, St. Anne's, associated with this world we long for, is in the East.

Hrossa call this kind of longing *wondelone*. They believe that when one dies, he is dropped like a stone in water back to the source, the center of life from which all comes: "Let it go down, sink, fall away. Once below the surface there are no divisions, no layers in the water yielding all the way down; all one and unwounded is that element. . . . Let it go down; the *hnau* rises from it. This is the second life, the other beginning. Open, oh coloured world, without weight, without shore. You are second and better; this was first and feeble."

Lewis believes that fairy stories and myth arouse this longing, giving the actual world a "new dimension of depth." This special kind of longing, says Lewis, is *"askesis,"* or a spiritual exercise. Since we long for another world, to see and be united with beauty, we create new worlds and new creatures, such as Malacandra and Perelandra, gods and goddesses, nymphs and elves, hrossa and eldila. Furthermore, such stories present to us a whole class of experiences we have never had before, thus *adding* to life and recovering our vision of the world.

Following closely the biblical account of the fall of man and the angels, Lewis's myth of Deep Heaven says that earth is a lonely and silent outcast from the solar system, controlled by an evil ruler who was once one of the angels himself. Despite the death and fear we have known all our lives, outside earth exists a world of order and beauty filled with light and living creatures engaged in a perpetual battle. The universe, which seems dark and chaotic to our modern minds, is also intricately ordered into a pattern that includes everything made, even you and me. Nevertheless, here on earth seeps an evil that has pervaded every area of our lives—even our feelings about and treatment of Nature—and reverberates throughout the entire universe.

As the Dark Shadow grows ever stronger, it threatens to become as dangerous as did the Tower of Babel centuries ago. Man seeks to become Lord of his world and the universe, to be greater than the God who exists and will not tolerate such evil to last forever. This God, who is not a vaporous spirit but a more solid reality than anything we have experienced, can unmake our world. But he has also provided a way out for man, his artwork, a copy of him, through what his Son did on Thulcandra many years ago. Maleldil's incarnation on earth is seen as the center of our history. Blood is the "substance wherewith Maleldil remade the worlds before any world was made" and through which he redeemed earth. According to the eldila, "In the Fallen World He prepared for Himself a body and was united with the Dust and made it glorious forever. This is the end and final cause of all creating, and the sin whereby it came is called Fortunate and the world where this was enacted is the centre of worlds." Because he has experienced sin itself, Ransom knows one reason why Maleldil came to earth, but the Green Lady knows another. And if a fall occurred on another planet,

Ransom knows that Maleldil would redeem it through some other and greater act of love or glory.

Great stirrings are now under way as the universe is dividing into two camps. We too must choose one side or the other. Maleldil's people on earth, members of a small company, are his tools to keep pushing back the spread of evil. But he will not wait long. Soon he will return to earth again so that the memory of the evil ruler and "that hideous strength" will be blotted out forever. Then earth will be restored to its place in the Great Dance, and the great bleeding wound from which each of us suffers will be eternally healed.

APPENDIX: A SUMMARY OF THE TRILOGY

The day of the fields of Arbol will fade and the
days of Deep Heaven itself are numbered. Not
thus is He great. He dwells (all of Him
dwells) within the seed of the smallest flower
and is not cramped: Deep Heaven is inside
Him who is inside the seed and does not
distend Him. Blessed be He!

The three books of the trilogy center chiefly upon Dr. Elwin Ransom, a philologist and fellow of Cambridge College, who is on a walking tour of England and seeking lodging for the night. He stumbles upon a cottage where a woman frantically is searching for her son Harry, who works at The Rise. Ransom agrees to seek him out and send him home. With many misgivings, Ransom proceeds to the old farmhouse where physicist Edward Rolles Weston and his assistant, Richard Devine, are preparing for a voyage to Malacandra (Mars). Weston's goal is for mankind to spread to other planets when earth is no longer fit for life. Four years ago they had visited the planet and were told by its ruling "angel," the

Oyarsa, to bring back a man if they wanted Malacandrian gold. So they kidnap Ransom onto the spaceship, first by a drugged drink, then by a knock on the head.

Though he is a prisoner, Ransom nevertheless experiences a joyous journey through space, finding it not cold and lifeless, but somehow "full" of life and radiant with intense light that rubs him with a new vitality and gives him a lightness of heart. But since Ransom overhears his captors speaking of how he is to be turned over to the "sorns," he determines to escape rather than face such supposedly monstrous creatures.

In twenty-eight days they reach Malacandra. Like his surprise at finding space different from what he had always imagined, he is amazed to find Malacandra a strangely bright, still, sparkling pastel world of pink and purple vegetation and pale blue sky. Weston and Devine seem about to turn him over to six unusually elongated and spindly creatures. But suddenly a shining beast with great snapping jaws flashes from the water and diverts their attention, allowing Ransom to flee.

Journeying aimlessly in search of food, Ransom encounters one of the creatures of the planet, a seallike hross named Hyoi. Hyoi takes him on an uncomfortable boat ride to his village in the lowlands of the planet. Thrilled at the discovery that the hrossa speak their own language, Ransom learns it and becomes acquainted with their customs and somewhat primitive, simple lifestyle. He learns that the Oyarsa rules the entire planet, but Maleldil the Young, who lives with the Old One, made the world. Malacandra has three rational and distinct species: hrossa are the seal- or otterlike poets and fishermen; scorns are the tall, spindly intelligentsia; pfifltriggi are froglike craftsmen and historians. There are also eldila, a superior kind of "hnau" (rational creature with a soul) that cannot be seen except as strange variations in the light.

While participating in a glorious attack on the hnakra, a deadly aquatic monster, Ransom and the hrossa are commanded by one of these eldila that Ransom must go to the Oyarsa. Instead, they first hunt the monster. As a result of their disobedience, Hyoi is killed by a shot from Weston and Devine. So Ransom, ashamed, is directed by a hross, Whin, to the tower of Augray, a sorn who lives in the steep, cold, almost airless *harandra* or highland. Ransom shares information about earth's geology, history, language, and science with an older sorn-scientist and his pupils. Then Augray carries him to Meldilorn, the dwelling-place of Oyarsa.

At the paradisal island of Meldilorn, Ransom waits until Oyarsa sends for him. Hordes of all three of the Malacandrian species begin to descend on the island. He studies the Malacandrian history carved in stone and has his own unattractive portrait chiseled in stone by a pfifltrigg. Called before the Oyarsa, Ransom hesitantly follows an avenue lined with creatures and eldila. From Oyarsa he learns the history of Deep Heaven and earth's sad state. Earth is "outside" Heaven and silent because its own Oyarsa became "bent." When Weston and Devine had been to Malacandra four years earlier, they were told they could not take the gold unless one of their race came to the Oyarsa—not for evil purposes, but so the Oyarsa could hear more about earth. Ransom, in fact, had been specifically "called" to the planet. In turn, Ransom tries to explain why Weston and Devine have really come to Malacandra—to spread the seed of mankind to other planets in case earth becomes uninhabitable and so man can become immortal.

Weston and Devine are brought struggling before the Oyarsa to be tried, along with three dead hrossa. Weston comically communicates in baby talk to an old hross he supposes is the Oyarsa, then tries to appease him with junk jewelry. Thus, the pfifltriggi and hrossa are ordered to soundly douse his head in water while the dead hrossa are "buried" or "unmade." When Weston returns, Ransom translates for him his speech to the Oyarsa about his goals of interplanetary travel and colonization. While Weston is merely "bent," concludes the ruler, Devine is totally "broken" by greed. Oyarsa gives them just ninety days to return to earth, after which the ship will become "unmade." Ransom chooses to return with them to earth, agreeing to carefully watch Weston and Devine for other evils they may do. For it is just the beginning of many comings and goings between worlds, a revolutionary celestial year of great changes.

Eldila surround and fill the ship on its journey back to earth. As the days click away, the sphere comes dangerously near the sun and its unbearable heat. With just two days left to reach earth and with the moon still between them and home, they resign themselves to sure death. Ransom is plunged into unconsciousness, awaking to the welcome patter of rain and the smell of the mud and grass of earth. Nine months after he left, he has returned home safely but greatly changed. He relates his story to his friend Lewis, who puts his story in fictional form.

Ransom is ill for three months. Then, in 1942, Maleldil summons him to Perelandra (Venus). The two "sides" in the battle between the good and bad eldila are appearing increasingly on earth, and earth's Bent Oyarsa is preparing an attack on Perelandra. Despite the temptation to do otherwise, Lewis comes at Ransom's request to help him prepare for his journey. Lewis nails the naked Ransom into a white, semi-transparent coffin that is transported to Perelandra by Malacandra's Oyarsa. Over a year later, he returns, glowing with health and seemingly ten years younger, joyfully relating to Lewis the following details of his trip:

Ransom awakens to find himself in an iridescent, "delicately gorgeous" world of warm green ocean swells, golden sky, and floating islands of vegetable matter, a world where he experiences a sense of excessive pleasure with no accompanying guilt. He encounters one of the two human inhabitants of this young planet—a Green Lady with unearthly calm in her face, who is totally pure and innocent and yet susceptible to evil. They skim over the waves on two dolphinlike fish to the "Fixed Land" to search for her husband the King, discovering only that Weston has landed on the planet in another spaceship. He has a "subtly unfamiliar" look in his face because, as the Bent Oyarsa's agent on Perelandra, he is possessed by the Devil. Furthermore, his philosophy has changed to a belief in emergent evolution—the idea that everything moves toward Spirit or Force.

Weston soon becomes totally taken over by the demon within him—an "Un-man"—and begins to not only tempt the Green Lady, but to destroy the vegetative and animal life of the planet. Maleldil has forbidden the Green Lady and the King to sleep on the "Fixed Land." This bidding is a strange one, the Un-man argues: Imagine what it would be like to live there; it would make you wiser, older, and to turn away from what I am telling you would be like rejecting the fruit you are given to eat at any one moment. Besides, Maleldil wants to make you "older" by letting go of your hand. Certainly the King would also like you better if you were older.

Day after day the banter continues. You are becoming your own. Maleldil *wants* you to disobey, but obviously cannot tell you this himself. The task is so difficult that only the courageous can succeed. Furthermore, because of the breaking of Maleldil's command on earth, Maleldil became a man and came to earth himself; so man's action was really "fortunate." Then the Un-man tells thousands of tragic stories of women who risked all for their husbands, children, and people.

The discussion goes on day after day, while all Ransom can do is to keep awake as much as possible and argue against the Un-man when he can. The most successful temptation, however, is the idea of doing a Great Deed for the King and Maleldil now before the chance slips away. Finally the Un-man introduces the Green Lady to the concept of self and vanity by adorning her in a robe of feathers and leaves which she can admire in his cheap and tiny mirror.

This can't go on, Ransom reasons to himself. Why doesn't a miracle occur on the side of good for a change? Then Ransom realizes *he* is the miracle, and everything depends on his action. What is worse, this action must not only be spiritual, but a *physical* warfare, for he had been chosen before the very creation of the world to do this deed and was thus named Ransom.

So the weak, sedentary philologist and the determined physicist batter each other until the Un-man flees limping into the sea and onto one of the dolphinlike fish. Bedraggled, shredded, and smarting with pain, Ransom pursues on his own fish for hours. He begins to be torn by doubts as to whether his task is really so urgent and important after all. Then Weston's real self seemingly returns long enough to argue that the real universe ends in death, that reality is irrational. Suddenly they are pulled down as they grapple with each other into swirling waters and deposited into a pitch-black underground cavern. Ransom pounds his foe seemingly to death, then awaits a daylight that never comes.

Realizing he must search for a way out or remain in darkness, Ransom climbs upward to a larger cave and to a still higher cavern lighted by a vast subterranean fire. There he sees the Un-man, still alive, and a hideous, many-legged creature. Once and for all, he smashes the Un-man in the face with a stone and hurls him into the fire in the name of the Father, Son, and Holy Ghost.

As he wanders aimlessly and hopelessly, Ransom sees evidence of a vast underground culture of beetlelike inhabitants. At last, he slips into a torrent of water and is gently returned to the outside world, moving from the cave of translucent rock into a pool high atop a mountain. For about three weeks he drinks in a glorious view of flower-covered glens, valleys, and mountaintops. He sleeps and recuperates, "breast-fed" by Venus in a sort of second infancy. His only real injury, he discovers, is a bleeding wound in the heel, inflicted at some time by the Un-man's bite. One day he chisels a memorial stone to Weston; two days later he descends the mountain, discovering the delightful "ripple-trees" and a marvelous singing beast. Finally, Ransom ascends a great mountain, feeling no fatigue and content to be forever climbing almost as a state of life.

Bid by Maleldil, Ransom goes from a pass between

two peaks bathed in red flowers to a secret valley with a small pool in the center. There lies the coffin ready for his return to earth. There also wait the Oyeresu of Malacandra and Perelandra, who appear to him in various awesome forms and inform him that this is the day when the King and Queen will at last ascend the throne of Perelandra. A Noah's ark of animals gradually floods the valley, and they line up in ceremony for the coming of the majestic King and Queen. These two glorious humans, the image of what Adam and Eve were meant to be, are given the planet to rule by the Oyarsa, who remains as their counsel and as a gift from Maleldil. Now they know evil, but not through falling into sin as did Adam and Eve. While the Green Lady was tempted, the King learned of it in Lur, where Maleldil showed him many things.

From this day, the couple will rule from Tai Harendrimar, the Hill of Life, and bear children. Beasts will talk. After 10,000 revolutions around the sun, the clouds will be ripped apart so Deep Heaven can be seen. Perelandrians will take on eldilic form. Maleldil will then descend to Thulcandra to blot out evil and cleanse it so that earth can be reunited to the heavens and know its *true* beginning. After this prophecy is told, the glorious song of the eldila begins, and Ransom receives a vision of the Great Dance itself. This ceremony on the mountain lasts one year. Finally, the King and Queen sadly help Ransom into the coffin, cover his eyes with red flowers, and bid him farewell until unconsciousness overtakes him.

Six years after the Malacandrian voyage began, the culmination of Ransom's story takes place on earth. *That Hideous Strength* follows the divergent paths of two lives, Jane and Mark Studdock. Married for just six months and already feeling pent in, Jane tries fruitlessly to complete work on a dissertation on John Donne. But she is haunted by memory of her dream of a "head" and the unearthing of an "ancient, British, druidical kind of man." She reads of the very same "head" in the newspaper—that of an Arab, Alcasan, guillotined for poisoning his wife. Skeptical and confused, she nevertheless confides in her tutor and his wife, the Dimbles, who perceive that her dreams are visions of real events and persuade her to see Grace Ironwood at St. Anne's. Though she is assured her dreams are real and will not go away, Jane is afraid of becoming involved and returns home, trying to close her mind to the whole affair.

Her husband, Mark, a fellow in sociology at Bracton College, has different problems. The National Institute of Co-ordinated Experiments (N.I.C.E.), with headquarters at Bel-bury, plans to buy Bragdon Wood from Bracton College in Edgestow. Its goals are fusion of state and applied scientific research; control of the environment and man's destiny; selective breeding; freeing man from body, birth, breeding, death, the organic, subjective; remedial treatment of crimi-nals; and placing Man Immortal on the throne of the universe using Nature as instrument.

Through a fellow member of the college, Feverstone (the very same Devine of *Out of the Silent Planet*), Mark is offered a nebulous position at N.I.C.E. He is taken to meet Wither, the Deputy Director, and attempts futilely to find out what exactly he is to do there. But N.I.C.E. is really in-terested in Jane, whose visions would be invaluable to them. Mark also meets Hingest, a scientist and former Bracton fellow; Filostrato, a scientist; and Fairy Hardcastle, head of the Women's Auxiliary Institutional Police. Yet everyone is strangely vague, secretive, and cold.

As N.I.C.E. begins its gradual takeover of Edgestow and seeps into nearby communities, the Dimbles are turned out of their home, and Hingest is mysteriously murdered on his attempted escape home. Still trying to establish what his duties are, Mark writes a report on Cure Hardy, a lovely but backward little village that N.I.C.E. plans to turn into a reser-voir, and writes propagandistic lies for the newspapers. He is torn between the N.I.C.E. job and his Bracton fellowship, driven always by a desire to be a member of the innermost circle of people.

Meanwhile, Jane meets with Camilla and Arthur

Denniston, Mark's former schoolmate, discovering they are members of a "company" at St. Anne's under the leadership of a Fisher-King. They are to fight a danger hanging over the human race. Jane refuses to join this company, but agrees to tell them her valuable dreams. Later, terrified after a vision about Merlin and of a man with a pince-nez (Frost) whom she encounters in real life on the street, she flees back to St. Anne's. The stagnant fog that has blanketed the town for days, just as the evil of N.I.C.E. has spread over the country-side, lifts just as she comes to the hilltop on which St. Anne's is perched. When she meets the Director, Ransom, the Fisher-King, her world is unmade. With all her defenses at last down, she learns that obedience is the true key to marriage. As she returns on the train, Jane is a changed woman, aware of the beauty of the world and, without vanity, her own beauty and uniqueness. On her way back to her home in San-down, she is arrested by the N.I.C.E. police and interrogated and molested by the Fairy. But on their drive back through town, mechanical problems allow Jane to escape and seek refuge at St. Anne's.

A valuable member of the "company," the skeptical MacPhee, relates Ransom's history to her. Ransom, who once traveled to Mars and Venus, is now directing a campaign against evil eldils under orders from good eldils, his Masters, from outer space. He is the Pendragon of Logres, who will never die or age and who suffers from a bleeding heel. Ransom fears that Belbury will join forces with the magical pow-ers of Merlin, a magician from the days of King Arthur, who lies entranced but ready to awaken under Bragdon Wood. He also suspects that dark eldilic power is behind the work of N.I.C.E.

While Jane has found her place at St. Anne's and with it peace and well-being, Mark is becoming more and more disenchanted with N.I.C.E. Drawn into the "Inner Ring" of Frost and Filostrato, he is taken before the disgusting Head itself. This greenish and slobbering head of Alcasan has been kept alive, supposedly, by a jungle of tubes and dials. When the Fairy tells him Jane isn't well, Mark fearfully hurries home. Of course, he only finds Jane gone and total disruption in Edgestow and nearby Courthampton. Indignant, Mark seeks out Dimble, who chastises him, yet charitably offers to help him to the "right side." Confused and simply wanting to mull things over, Mark is arrested falsely by N.I.C.E. police for Hingest's murder.

Dimble, in the meantime, returns home only to be sent out again with Jane and Arthur Denniston to search for Merlin on a dark and dripping night. They are guided only by Jane's vision and find nothing but glimpses of a fire, a tramp, and a man on a horse. Meanwhile, N.I.C.E. picks up the tramp, believing he is Merlin and that he cannot speak English. Over the next few days, they present a comic parade of experts in various languages before him with no success. The real Merlin appears in all his grandeur at St. Anne's and casts all but Ransom into an enchanted sleep. Eldilic powers are now beginning to descend to earth because man tried to enter Deep Heaven. They will work through Merlin, the one man whose mind is open to be invaded because he once used white magic.

Wither and Frost plot to draw Mark "in" to the true core of Belbury by giving him objectivity training. Faced now with the possibility of death as a prisoner, Mark realizes he has been a lifelong fool and should have recognized the true nature of N.I.C.E. and his colleagues from the start. All his life, the yearning to be a member of the Inner Ring had made him eat and drink what he didn't like, associate with detestable people. At last now he is free from all constraints to be drawn in.

Even Frost appears to him in his true colors; his "program" is to reduce all emotion and subjectivity in Mark. The only choice is thus to be destroyed or be admitted to the Inner Ring. The old excitement returns for a moment as Frost educates Mark to the goals of N.I.C.E.: reduction of subjectivity, sixteen major wars to reduce the population, the individual all "head" and the race all technocracy. The real Head is Macrobes (evil eldils) who merely work through Alcasan's cortex and vocal organs. Mark is placed in the distorted and grotesquely decorated Objective Room, which only has the opposite effect of making him conscious of the Normal. He also is given guard duty over the tramp and is amused to secretly discover that the tramp really knows English and believes his hosts are odd foreigners.

Meanwhile, Jane and Mrs. Dimble prepare the lodge for the reunion of newlyweds Ivy Maggs, Jane's former maid, and her husband, arrested for petty theft. There Jane has a bewildering encounter with the earthly wraith of Venus, the goddess of love, and her romping dwarves. This is only the prelude to the descent on St. Anne's of the real gods: Mercury, who creates punning and witty use of language; Venus, with her fragrant and romantic drowsiness; Mars, who instills a fighting spirit; Saturn, with a coldness and heavy pressure; and at last Jupiter the King, with pomp and festivity.

Back at N.I.C.E., however, the dark eldils wreak vengeance on their own people. Merlin poses as a Basque priest and expert in language, casting the bewildered tramp into a hypnotic trance and thereby gaining entrance to the heart of Belbury. At the inaugural banquet, Director Jules addresses the audience, but his words begin to slowly disintegrate into nonsense. Wither, who tries futilely to restore order to the hysterically laughing audience, also begins to babble. The crowd soon disrupts into a chaos of shouting and frantic running about. The Fairy shoots Jules and is herself mauled by a tiger, the first of an endless menagerie of angry animals loosed upon the room. Merlin sends Mark on to St. Anne's.

Controlled now by the Macrobes, Filostrato, Wither, and their pupil, the mad preacher Straik, go before the Head and bow down in worship. Filostrato is beheaded, Straik stabbed, and Wither mutilated by a bear. Frost locks himself in the Objective Room, sets it on fire, and dies, at last aware that there is such a thing as self and responsibility. Feverstone casually watches the show in the banquet hall to its bloody end. Stealing a car, he is forced to drive on madly and recklessly by his stowaway Merlin, overturns, and is swallowed into the earth. A mass exodus from Edgestow precedes its destruction by earthquakes, shocks, and floods. But this is only one of many Edgestows that will be destroyed before Maleldil returns to earth to wipe out evil once and for all.

Until then, the company of Logres at St. Anne's, as well as similar "companies" of each country, must persist in pushing out the evil that continues to creep back in until the end times. In celebration, the group at St. Anne's dress in festal robes for the final dinner, for Ransom is to return tomorrow to Perelandra to be at last healed of his wound. Mark and Jane are reunited in the lodge prepared for the Maggs—Jane now humble and obedient as a wife, Mark now more sensitive as a lover, and both now aware of the Normal and Straight in their lives.

THE LANGUAGES IN THE TRILOGY

Old Solar

There was originally one common speech for all rational creatures of the planetary system except earth, where it was lost because of the fall. This speech is known as *Hlab-Eribol-ef-Cordi.* Now there is no human language in the world descended from it. But it is the language of the hrossa *(Hressa-Hlab),* of Perelandra, and of Numinor, and was known in fragments by old magicians of the Atlantean Circle who repeated it to initiates.

The words of Old Solar are polysyllabic and sound as if they are not "words at all but present operations of God, the planets, and the Pendragon." For this is the language spoken "before the Fall and beyond the Moon and the meanings were not given to the syllables by chance, or skill, or long tradition but truly inherent in them. . . . This was Language herself." Thus, the names Lewis uses for the planets, except Thulcandra, are said to be their *real* names.

In a letter, Lewis says there is no *obvious* connection between phonetic elements of Old Solar and actual language. However, he was familiar with Anglo-Saxon, Norse, Greek, Hebrew, and Latin. Lewis also felt fantasy names should be beautiful, suggestive, and strange; "spelling counts," he said, as much as sound. He also admitted that he liked to play with syllables and fit them together by ear to see if he could come up with pleasing new words with emotional, not intellectual, suggestiveness.

Malacandrian

Lewis noted that use of the words *har* (mountains) and *sorn/seroni,* which declined like *hoken* in Arabic, and *handramit,* which resembles *handhramaut* in Arabic, "are all accidents I knew nothing of," but show how hard it is to invent something that does not already exist.

All three Malacandrian hnau speak the same language—the speech of the hrossa (*Hressa-Hlab* or Old Solar), but also speak their own, less ancient tongues at home.

Hrossan Rules and Vocabulary

Very similar to Old Norse with its initial *h; h* disappears after *c.* Has suffixes and prefixes.

Has no words for forgive, shame, fault. Speech cannot be translated into English.

Hrossa have "furry" names.

ahihra   exclamation (proclaimed when Jupiter rises)

bent   evil

cordi   field

crah   last part of poem

ef   of

eribol   arbol (variation)

handra   land, earth (element)

handramit   low ground, watered country, gorge, canyon

harandra   high ground

hlab   language

Hleri   Hyoi's wife

hluntheline   crave something wrongly

hmān/hmāna   man

hnakra/hnéraki   aquatic sea monster

hnakrapunt   *hnakra* slayer

hnau/nau   rational being with spirit

Hnohra   gray-muzzled, venerable hross who teaches Ransom Old Solar

Hnoo   *hross* who dips Weston's head in water

honodraskud   edible pink weed on *handramit*

Hressa-Hlab   *hrossan* language

Hrikki   she-*hross* (cub) who talks to an eldil

Hrinha   *hross* in charge of ferry to Meldilorn

hross/hrossa   (feminine form *hressni*) one of three intelligent races on Malacandra

hru   blood (*Arbol hru:* gold)

Hyahi   Hyoi's brother

Hyoi   first *hross* to meet Ransom; murdered by Weston and Devine

pfifltriggi   one of three intelligent races on Malacandra

punt   kill

punti   slayers

sorn/séroni   one of three intelligent races on Malacandra

thulc silent

Urendi Maleldil a blessing

Whin *hross* who hunts *hnakra* with Hyoi and Ransom

wondelone to long for something such as joy; *Sehnsucht*

Pfifiltriggian

Pfifltriggian language is reminiscent of Turkish or Eastern. Myths of Australian aborigines give similar names, such as Kilpuruna, Purukupali, and Wuriupranala. Pfifltriggi speak mainly through their art. Their names are as follows:

Firikitekila in charge of cisterns at Meldilorn

Kalakaperi

Kanakaberaka carves Ransom's picture in stone

Parakataru

Tafalakeruf

Surnibur (Sorn Language)

Surnibur is a relatively modern speech, developed probably within our Cambrian period. It is "big sounding," can be translated, and has a different vocabulary than hrossan. Typical names are:

Arkal

Augray sorn who takes Ransom to Meldilorn

Belmo

Falmay

A DICTIONARY OF DEEP HEAVEN

After each entry, the book in which the word or name appears is abbreviated in parentheses as follows:

OSP *(Out of the Silent Planet)*
P *(Perelandra)*
THS *(That Hideous Strength)*

Many word definitions are from the *Oxford English Dictionary,* indicated as *(OED).* An asterisk *(*)* preceding a word signifies a relevant entry in the Dictionary under that (or a closely similar) heading.

Abhalljin (THS) (*see* **Aphallin, Avalon**) From *abhal* (Irish for apple).

Agrippa (THS) von Nettesheim. 15-16th c. German student of alchemy. Lewis's example of a magician.

Alcasan, François (THS) Distinguished Arab radiologist who poisoned his wife and was executed. His "Head" used by *N.I.C.E. Lewis may have based him on experiments of Dr. Alexis Carrel and Charles A. Lindbergh to keep a heart alive when removed from the body.

allegory (P) In the Preface to *Perelandra,* Lewis says the characters in the book are purely fictitious and none are allegorical. An allegory is an extended form of metaphor in which persons, objects, events "represent" or "stand for" abstract meanings.

Anti-Christ   Person opposed to Christ whose coming is described in Revelation 13 and 19. The *Un-man is in many ways reminiscent of him because he is the representative of *Satan, comes "out of" the sea, is wounded and thrown into a lake of fire.

Aphallin (THS)   (*see* **Abhalljin, Avalon**) From *aphal* (Old High German for apple).

Arbol (OSP, P)   The sun. Associated with gold in mythology. Perhaps derived from *aurum* (Latin for gold) and *sol* (Latin for sun).

Archimago (THS)   Chief magician, enchanter, great wizard who Spenser uses as personification of hypocrisy and Lewis cites as an example of a magician.

Argus (THS)   Mythological person with 100 eyes. Slain by Mercury, who in myth is known as "Argus queller."

Artemis (P, THS)   Virgin goddess Diana of the moon and hunt. We are told the *Green Lady might run like her, that her mild shafts are swift and painless.

Arthur (THS)   Probably a 5th c. Welsh or Roman military leader of the Celts in Wales against Germanic invaders. He eventually became a heroic legend. Lewis says he was a Christian general trained in Roman technique who almost succeeded in pulling society together.

Ask (P)   King of *Perelandra. Ask ("Ash") and *Embla ("Vine") are the first man and woman in Norse mythology.

Atlantean Circle (THS)   *Merlin and his magic are from the old Atlantean Circle. Some suggest this is Edenic power; others suggest the Atlantis myth. In a letter, Lewis states this was a pure invention, filling the same purpose in his narrative as "noises off" would in a stage play.

Augray (OSP)   *Sorn who lives in a tower, has a telescope, and leads *Ransom to *Meldilorn. *Aug* means open-eyed, sight in Old Norse. *Auge (OED)* means height, top, summit.

Avalon (THS)   (*see* **Abhalljin, Aphallin**) Island on *Perelandra where dwell *Enoch, *Elias, *Moses, *Melchisedec. *Ransom's wounds are to be healed there (cf. Frodo in *Lord of the Rings*). The tradition began with Wace and Layamon that *Arthur was transported to the Isle of Avalon (associated with Celtic Elysium) to be cured of his wounds, stands in perpetual guard over England, and will return when needed. Geoffrey of Monmouth believed the name came from *Aval* (apple)—the Island of Apples, or Paradise. Thus, Lewis may derive his alternate names Abhalljin and Aphallin from the root word apple: *Aphal* means apple in Old High German; *Abhal* means apple in Irish. Concerning sources of elements in the trilogy, Lewis said, "On the Tir-na'an Og element you hit the bull." Tir-na'an Og was the Celtic Elysium with a fountain of youth, healing balsam, and life-giving fruit.

B. (P)   Said to be present during conversation with Ransom and an anthroposophist. Stands for Owen Barfield, Lewis's friend for many years. He is mentioned later by Ransom—"It is one of Barfield's ancient unities"—to explain the relationship between Bultitude and Pinch, who have no distinction between affection and the physical. Anthroposophy is a religious philosophy based on the teachings of Rudolf Steiner, with doctrines such as the idea that all ideas are part of one larger, extrapersonal process; and that human consciousness has evolved in a unique way and will reach its culmination when man becomes more aware of his imagination, especially inner revelation and inspiration.

Babel (THS)   Great tower made of bricks in the plain of Chaldea. This story is paralleled by the goals of *N.I.C.E. and the confounding of their speech to gibberish. In their biography of Lewis, Hooper and Green say Lewis acknowledged his debt to Gordon Bottomley's poem "Babel" for the banquet at *Belbury.

Bacon, Sir Francis (THS)   Seventeenth-century essayist and scientist, one of the "founders" of empirical scientific method. In *The Abolition of Man,* Lewis says Bacon wanted to "extend man's power to the performance of all things possible"; his goal is that of magician.

Balinus (THS)   *Merlin says Jane *Studdock has done in *Logres a thing of which no less sorrow shall come than came of Balinus' stroke. Balin the Savage gave the *Fisher-King of myth a "dolorous blow," usually said to be in the thigh. In Charles *Williams, Balin also is said to have wounded King Pelles (Keeper of the Hallows), which prevented the union of Carbonek and Logres and therefore the coming of the Grail.

Balki (OSP)   Pool and waterfall (the Mountain of Water) surrounded by steep walls with holy images in them; called the "place of most awe" in all worlds. Since *hnéraki are found in the water, death, says the *hrossa, is in the pool. If this water is drunk, one dies (goes to *Maleldil).

Barbarossa, Frederick I (THS) (1123?-1190) King of Germany and the Holy Roman Empire.

Barfield (THS) Owen Barfield. (*see* **B.**)

Baron Corvo (THS) Jackdaw or crow of *St. Anne's menagerie. *Corvo* means pertaining to crow or raven *(OED)*.

Baru (P) King of *Perelandra. Based on the Hebrew verb involved in the idea, "in the image of God he created them."

Baru'ah (P) *Green Lady. (*see* **Baru**)

Belbury (THS) Headquarters of *N.I.C.E. Edwardian mansion, designed after Versailles, housing Blood Transfusion Office. *Bel* is the Babylonian form of Baal—any local fertility and nature god worshiped by ancient semitic people. *Bury,* of course, means to hide or conceal. In their biography of Lewis, Hooper and Green believe Belbury's taking over *Edgestow is based on the controversy over the founding of an atomic factory of Harwell near Blewbury, 15 minutes from Oxford.

bent (OSP) *Hrossan word for evil. Also used by J. R. R. Tolkien. Suggests deflected, inclined in some direction, a mental inclination, bias, as well as the possibility of correction, but usually the corruption of original good. Possibly derived from Augustine's *curvatus* (sin).

Bent One (OSP) (*see* **Thulcandra, Black Archon, Satan**) Lucifer, a rebel angel, also called the *Dark Archon, Bent *Oyarsa, Evil One. In a letter, Lewis says he is Satan. Greater and brighter than *Malacandra's Oyarsa, he desired to be like *Maleldil and became "bent."

Bernardus Silvestris (OSP) 15th c. medieval Platonist who wrote *De Mundi Universitate*. Lewis mentions him frequently in *The Discarded Image*. Coined the word Usiarch/Ousiarches.

Bill the Blizzard (THS) (*see* **Hingest**)

Black Archon (P)   (*see* **Bent One, Satan**) The *Oyarsa of earth. The Bible calls *Satan the "ruler of this world." The Greek word for ruler is *archon*.

Blaise (THS)   *Merlin's master. A fictional learned clerk who, according to legend, is said to be Merlin's master from birth.

blue (THS)   (*see* **colors**) Lewis makes a point of telling us that *Ransom's room and robe are blue, the traditional color of divine revelation (the sky is associated with the heavens), martyrdom, and *Mercury (language).

Bracton College (THS)   Small college within the University of *Edgestow. Founded in 1300 for the support of 10 learned men whose duties were to pray for the soul of Henry de Bracton, a lawyer, and to study the laws of England. Now has 40 fellows, including Mark *Studdock.

Bragdon Wood (THS) Wood near *Bracton College where *Merlin's Well is located. Old as Britain itself, it has a life of its own which is unchanged by time. Name has only accidental similarity to Bracton, but the Bracton family took advantage of this and said the wood belonged to the college. Based on Broceliande Wood (sea wood that leads to Heaven) of Charles *Williams. In a letter, Lewis notes how Bragdon Wood is similar to a grove at Magdalen College, where he taught.

Britain (THS)   (*see* **Logres**)

Brizeacre (THS)   *Edgestow psychiatrist. *Brize* is a form of "breeze" *(OED)*.

Broad (THS)   Neighbor of *St. Anne's whose horses perpetually romp through the garden.

Brobdingnag (THS)   Giant country in Swift's *Gulliver's Travels*. Jane *Studdock describes the hugeness of God pressing on her to something from Brobdingnag.

bubble-trees (P)   Trees that produce bubbles which are as reflective as glass and give a freshness and clarity of vision. Draw moisture from ocean and expel it, along with own sap, on land.

Bultitude (THS)   *St. Anne's bear, last of *Seven Bears of

Logres. Likes Ivy *Maggs and *Ransom the most. Has "no prose in his life." In a letter, Lewis mentions a Bultitude who is a bear at Whipsnade Zoo. Lewis's brother wrote that "a delightful brown plethoric" bear sat up and saluted for buns and that Jack had the dream of adding a pet bear to their own private menagerie which he intended to christen Bultitude. Bultitude is also the dignified father in Frederick Anstey's *Vice Versa,* a book Lewis owned and mentions in *Surprised by Joy* and "On Science Fiction." In another letter, Lewis says he made up the idea of the Seven Bears of Logres on analogy with the Nine Worthies or the Celtic Triads.

Busby, James (THS)   Bursar of *Bracton, former clergyman; large, with bushy black beard. Common name of some antiquity *(OED).*

Canaglia (THS)   Those outside *N.I.C.E., a word used by *Filostrato and the others. From *canalia,* a contemptuous name for the populace, mob *(OED).*

Carbonek (THS)   In Charles *Williams's *Taliessin Through Logres,* the castle in which the Grail is kept.

Carey (THS)   Mark *Studdock's former undergraduate friend.

Carstairs (THS)   Like *Hingest, liquidated by *N.I.C.E.

Cassibelaun (THS)   One of the *Pendragons. Mentioned by Geoffrey of Monmouth in *History of the Kings of England* as Cassibelaunus. Replaced his older brother Lud as King of England and fought Julius Caesar.

Churchwood (THS)   *Northumberland lecturer known by *Dimble who preached but did not practice the impossibility of ethics.

colors (THS)   In mythology, each planet was represented by a color. Similarly, each of the women at *St. Anne's puts on a robe especially suited for her for the final banquet. Ivy *Maggs's is green (associated with Nature, ivy); Camilla *Denniston's is steel (associated with dignity; in Virgil, Camilla is the huntress, and the moon, also the huntress, is associated with silver); Jane *Studdock's (like *Ransom's) is blue (associated with *Mercury and thus language, divine revelation); Mother *Dimble's is flame-colored (associated with *Venus); Grace *Ironwood's is black (associated with *Saturn); *Merlin's robe is red (associated with *Mars, war).

Compton (THS) Murdered by *N.I.C.E.

Conington (THS) Former *Bractonian who had lost his job.

Cosser (THS) Member of *N.I.C.E. sociology department who tricks Mark *Studdock into writing up report on *Cure Hardy. Freckle-faced with a wisp of black moustache and noncommittal eyes. A *cosser* is a dealer, barterer, bargainer *(OED)*.

Courthampton (THS) Village near *Belbury where Mark *Studdock hopes to catch a bus.

crah (OSP) (*see* **wondelone, hluntheline**) *Hrossan word for the last part of a poem. The hross makes the point that remembering and enjoying are one experience, just as the last part of the poem is one with the rest of the work.

Crowe, Richard (THS) Learned and saintly man killed by a musket at *Merlin's Well by troopers during a past skirmish.

Cunnigham (THS) Eighty-year-old man arrested by *N.I.C.E.

Curdie Books (THS) Children's books *The Princess and Curdie* and *The Princess and the Goblin* by George MacDonald, whose works Lewis greatly admired. Lewis first discovered the idea of "holiness" by reading MacDonald's *Phantastes*. The Curdie books are mentioned several times in *THS;* *Ransom, for example, says he lives, like the King in Curdie, on bread and wine.

Cure Hardy (THS) Ozana le Coeur Hardi, the anachronistic village which *N.I.C.E. plans on turning into a reservoir. Beauty spot with 16th c. almshouses; population mainly agricultural laborers and small rentiers. Lewis says it is part of Arthurian history. Osenain, called Ozanna le Cure Hardy in Malory, is one of 42 knights who ride to the aid of Leodegan (father of both Guineveres), besieged by Rion and pagan hosts and rescued by *Arthur's forces.

Curry (THS) Sub-warden of *Bracton and college politician who claims all he wants to do is research in military history. Leader of the *Progressive Element. After *Edgestow is destroyed, sees himself as sole survivor and future founder of a new college. *Curry* means to flatter ("curry favor") *(OED)*.

Daisy (THS) Member of *W.A.I.P.

Danae (OSP)   Mistress of *Zeus whom the god visited with a shower of gold. *Ransom feels like a second Danae as he travels through space.

Dark Eldila (THS)   Angels who became bent and followed the *Black Archon; similar to devils. Tellurian *eldila who are the reason for the fatal bent of earth's history.

Dark Tower, The   Fragment of a story about time-traveling (available in *The Dark Tower and Other Stories*) which Lewis may have begun as a sequel to *Out of the Silent Planet*.

de Brolie (THS)   Louis Victor de Broglie, who won Nobel Prize in Physics in 1929.

Deep Heaven (P)   Outer space.

Denniston, Arthur (THS)   Mark *Studdock's former friend and competition for the *Bracton fellowship. *Distributivist; said to be likely to end up in a monastery. Member of *St. Anne's company. He and his wife like "Weather." Name "Arthur" significant, for he probably will become the next *Pendragon of *Logres.

Denniston, Camilla (THS)   Tall, forthright, valiant; member of *St. Annes. Carries the future of *Logres in her body (her child will be a future *Pendragon). Camilla in Virgil is a huntress fleet of foot or riding, just as Lewis's Camilla is described as "so straight, so forthright, so valiant, so fit to be mounted on a horse, so divinely tall." Camilla is also a character (Scudamour's fiancée) in Lewis's *The *Dark Tower*.

Devine, Dick (OSP)   Richard *Feverstone in THS. *Ransom admired him as a boy, then found him a bore who mocked cliches of his elders. Attended Wedenshaw, then Cambridge, then received Leicester fellowship. Accompanies *Weston to *Malacandra out of greed for gold. The *Oyarsa says his hnau is dead and he is only a talking animal; only greed is left, so he is broken, not bent. In *THS*, he gets Mark *Studdock his fellowship; is fellow of *Bracton, *N.I.C.E. member, emergency governor of *Edgestow, member of Parliament. Tries to stay on both sides. Has long, straight nose, clenched teeth; hard, bony face; hates country, weather, and walking. After *Merlin forces him to drive a stolen car into a ditch, he is swallowed up in an earthquake. Humphrey Carpenter believes Lewis may be basing him on his Magdalen College foe Harry Weldon, because Devine calls Mark an "incurable romantic." Devine probably satire on "divine."

Dew, Tony (THS)   "Dark little man from the bank."

Dimble, Cecil (THS)   Aging fellow of *Northumberland, Jane *Studdock's tutor, member of *St. Anne's. Knows *Arthurian history and *Old Solar. In a letter, Lewis says he is a literary critic. Seems to express Lewis's feelings as a tutor who must go hear a dull pupil present an essay on Swift beginning "Swift was born." Robert Reilly suggests he is based on Tolkien because a big beech tree is destroyed in Dimble's garden (in *Tree and Leaf,* Tolkien laments the tearing down of a poplar tree).

Dimble, Margaret (THS)   Mother Dimble, Cecil's wife of 30 years. An "aunt" to all Cecil's pupils. Humorous, easy-natured, childless, prays, member of *St. Anne's. A fertility or "mother symbol." *Dimble* is an attribute of obscurity or gloom *(OED)*.

distributivist (THS)   An economic program advocated by G. K. Chesterton calling for the widest possible distribution of private property, where everyone would own his own small farm, shop, or factory.

Donne (THS)   John Donne, 17th c. metaphysical poet (1572-1631), known for his frank love poetry and shocking use of metaphors called conceits. Ironically, Jane *Studdock, who refuses to have children, is attempting to write her dissertation on Donne's glorification of the body.

Doyle, Father (THS)   *Stone's assistant in searching for *Merlin; knows Latin; called a "sound colleague." *Doyle* is an obsolete form of dole, divided *(OED)*.

Duncanson (THS)   *MacPhee's uncle; Moderator of the Scottish General Assembly who would always say, "Show it to me in the Word of God."

Dunne (THS)   J. W. Dunne wrote *An Experiment With Time* (1927). Mark *Studdock refers to him with reference to time.

dynamism (P)   *Weston's philosophy of reaching forward toward Spirit (God).

earth (OSP, P, THS) (*see* **Silent Planet**; also **Thulcandra, Tellus**) The *Oyarsa of earth became bent and wanted to be like *Maleldil. To avoid spreading his evil to *Deep Heaven, Maleldil confined him and his eldila to earth, where they have made their headquarters. Wanting to make war on Deep Heaven, the Bent Oyarsa works through bent men. Maleldil promised he would not send powers to mend or mar earth until the end times, but when men sent spaceships to spread sin, the barrier was broken and now eldila from Deep Heaven can invade earth. Earth is shown to be dead, silent, cloudlike, a waste-space, heavy with gravity (sin), an enemy-occupied territory in a state of siege.

Edgestow (THS) Country college village. In Preface to *THS*, Lewis says it has no resemblance (save for smallness) to Durham, the only university with which he had pleasant associations. Durham is the beautiful town where Durham University is located. Edgestow is destroyed by fires and earthquakes. *Edgestow* seems to be associated with the idea of a frontier (between Logres and Britain).

eldil, eldila (OSP, P, THS) (*see* **Oyarsa**) Angels who inhabit space. Superior intelligences; do not eat, breed, breathe, or die; have bodies different from planetary animals (light goes through them). There are both good and bad eldila (Tellurian or *dark eldila), engaged in invisible warfare. Oyeresu are the greatest of eldila. In two letters, Lewis says eldila are angels, whom he believes are actual beings. If they have the same relation to pagan gods that they do in *Perelandra, then they might really manifest themselves in divine form as they do to *Ransom. Lewis also says eldila are not meant to be fairies. According to Humphrey Carpenter, Tolkien thought the eldila were inspired by the Eldar (three kindreds of elves) in *The Silmarillion*. *Eld* is Norwegian for fire, flame; *eld* also comes from English *elder* and German *alt* (old); Anglo-Saxon *eald* means chief, old, eminent and *ealdor* means chief, prince, lord; *engill* is Old Norse for angel; and *engil* is Old High German for angel.

Elias (THS) Elijah. Prophet carried into Heaven without dying (2 Kings 2:1ff.). Said to be with *Melchisedec, *Enoch, *Moses, and *Arthur in *Abhalljin/Aphallin.

Eloi, Eloi, lama sabachthani (P) Words spoken by Christ on the cross: "My God, my God, why hast thou forsaken me?" (Matt. 27:46; Mk. 15:34). Yelled by the *Un-man during his argument that martyrs are not helped, just as Christ was not rescued from the cross. Reveals that *Weston is *Satan, who was present at the crucifixion.

Elwin (OSP)   *Ransom's first name, which means "friend of the *eldila," one befriended by the elves (Anglo-Saxon). According to Humphrey Carpenter, from Tolkien's Aelfwine (elf-friend).

Embla (P)   *Green Lady. *Ask ("Ash") and Embla ("Vine") are the first man and woman in Norse mythology.

Enoch (THS)   Lived 365 years, then God took him (he did not die) (Gen. 5:18ff.; Heb. 11:5). Said to be with *Melchisedec, *Elias, *Moses, and *Arthur in *Abhalljin/Aphallin.

Fairy (THS)   (*see* **Hardcastle**)

Faustus (THS)   Marlowe's Dr. Faustus is referred to by Lewis as an example of an old magician and ceremonial scientist. In *The Abolition of Man*, Lewis says Faustus does not have a thirst for knowledge, but a desire for "gold and guns and girls."

fellows of Bracton (THS)   There are 40 fellows, including *Feverstone, *Glossop, *Hingest, *Pelham, *Raynor, *Sancho, *Studdock, *Ted, *Telford, and *Watson.

Felix Peccatum Adae (P)   (*see* **Fortunate Fall**)

Feverstone, Lord (THS)   (*see* **Devine, Dick**) *Fever* plus *stone* is a strange combination, which could represent his desire to be on both sides (*Bracton and *Belbury) or else his "fever" for gold in *OSP*.

Field of Arbol (P)   Solar system.

Filostrato, Professor (THS)   Great physiologist who believes it is he who kept the Head alive. Fat Italian eunuch. In a letter, Lewis says he is the next best scientist after *Hingest because he is not inside the *Belbury circle. Has a treble voice; huge, dark, smooth face; black hair; foreign accent. Guillotined in the laboratory by *Straik and *Wither. Boccaccio's nickname was il Filostrato ("one laid low by love").

Fisher-King (THS)   *Ransom in *THS*. Name bequeathed to him by his sister in India when she died. Title of the master of knights of the Holy Grail in medieval legend; also keeper of the Grail. Suffers from an unhealing wound (usually in the thigh, received from *Balin the Savage). The land has become waste, but will be restored when he is returned to his youthful vigor and beauty. Also associated with

Christian fish *(Ichthys)* symbol. First appeared in Chretien, as well as Malory, as Pellam, the Maimed King. (*See* Jessie Weston, *From Ritual to Romance.*)

Fisher-King, Mrs. (THS)   Ransom's sister who left Ransom a fortune and her name. Friend of *Sura; married; lived in India. In some versions of the story, the Grail was last seen in India's Sarras region.

Fixed Land (P)   (*see* **floating islands**) Solid ground on *Perelandra with mountain, rocks, pillars, stream, and great silence. King and Queen commanded not to sleep or stay here, but to return to floating islands. Could represent desire for security and man's will rather than conformity to God's. After King and Queen are given rule of Perelandra, we learn that the purpose of the Fixed Land was to lead them to their destined throne and on to the splendor of *Maleldil.

floating islands (P)   (*see* **Fixed Land**) Coppery islands on *Perelandra made of matted vegetation that change shape with the water. The King and Queen are commanded to stay and sleep here rather than on Fixed Land. Thus, the islands could represent conformity to the will of God, no matter what the conditions, and living by faith. Lewis got this image from Olaf *Stapledon's *Last and First Men.*

Fortunate Fall (P)   *"Felix Peccatum Adae."* The argument (used by *Un-man) that the fall of man was "fortunate" because it allowed Christ to come to earth.

Frost, Augustus (THS)   Psychiatrist at *N.I.C.E. Has pince-nez, pointed beard, regular features, bright Arctic smile, extreme white forehead. Has become like a "hard, bright little needle," with no passions or motives left, because he believes these to be merely the result of chemical phenomena. Before he dies, he learns that souls and personal responsibility do exist. Under influence of *Dark Eldila, he burns himself and the *Objective Room. Name *Frost* suggestive of his cold objectivity and frozen emotions. In *The Abolition of Man,* Lewis's image of the modern scientist is "a mild-eyed scientist in pince-nez." In "Reply to Professor *Haldane" *(Of Other Worlds),* Lewis says Frost is the mouthpiece of Professor *Waddington's ethical theories. He also says Frost worships the *Macrobes: "No man at present is (probably) doing what I represent Frost as doing: but he is the ideal point at which certain lines of tendency already observable will meet if produced."

Garden of Hesperides (P)   Mythological garden of Atlas containing tree with golden apples guarded by a dragon. *Ransom likens the garden on *Perelandra to this because of the tiny dragon encircling the fruit tree.

Gilly, Aunt (THS)   Mark *Studdock's aunt. *Gilly* comes from *gillic,* a giddy young woman *(OED).*

Glossop (THS)   *Bracton fellow who feels *Feverstone should not have a fellowship since he is away too much.

Glundandra (THS)   (*see* **Jupiter**) Glund, Glund-Oyarsa, Jupiter. Means "king" (Glund-Oyarsa). In a letter, Lewis says he chose the name to suggest the heaviness of the huge planet.

Golden Bough (THS)   Work by Sir James Frazer (1890; 12 volumes 1911-15) containing anthropological examples of the primitive motif of slaying the king for the tribe. Sees *magic as a pseudo-science by which primitive man attempts to control Nature. Magic reminds *Wither of this book.

Great Worlds (OSP)   Planets outside the Asteroids.

green (P)   The King and Queen of *Perelandra are both green. In a letter, Lewis says he could not see *Tor and *Tinidril as anything but green, but was afraid of the effect it would have on others' minds. *Venus is the name for the tincture green when the names of the planets are used in blazonry *(OED).*

Green Lady (P)   (*see* **Green**) *Tinidril, *Baru'ah, *Embla, *Yatsurah are her other names. An Eve-figure, like a goddess, with utter innocence and yet liable to succumb to temptation. In a letter, Lewis says it was almost impossible to write about such a character whom the fall put poles apart—pagan goddess and virgin—but it was worth doing if he could do a fraction of it.

Grip (THS)   Mark *Studdock's childhood society, an *Inner Ring of athletic heroes. "Grip" suggests the hold an Inner Ring has on a person like Mark.

Guinevere (THS)   Wife of King *Arthur who presides with him over his court, but is unfaithful with Lancelot, who later saves her from burning at the stake. Retires to a convent.

Haeckel, Ernst H. (THS)   German biologist and natural philosopher read by *Jules. Built upon the concept of evolution a doctrine of material monism: matter is the one fundamental reality; therefore, the universe is a single material substance.

Haldane, J. B. S.   (1892-1964) World famous physiologist, biochemist, biologist, geneticist, philosopher, Marxist, and spokesman of science. Lewis was influenced by his collection of essays called *Possible Worlds: A Scientist Looks at Science* in the writing of *THS*. Haldane believed man will colonize other planets, solve problems only by application of the scientific method, must control evolution (including his own); that there is no afterlife; that experimentation with animals is necessary. In his essay "Auld Hornie, F. R. S." (found in *Shadows of Imagination*, ed. Mark Hillegas), he criticizes Lewis's trilogy. Lewis's reply is found in *Of Other Worlds*. Haldane is possibly represented by *Weston.

handra (OSP)   *Hrossan word for land. Serves as a suffix (when the initial *h* is removed) for such words as *Malacandra and *Perelandra. Probably from *land* plus *terra* (Latin for earth).

handramit (OSP)   *Hrossan word for low ground. *Handra* means land in *Hrossan; suffix *mit* means low in Old Norse. *Handramits* appear as geometric canals which were engineered after the *Bent One of earth smote the *harandras* and made them cold and unfit for life, thus releasing warmth to keep the planet alive. These can be compared to "canals" seen on *Mars which people traditionally believed were engineered by its inhabitants. Hrossa live in the *handramits*. A *hadramaut* is an area in Arabia; there is also a *handhramaut* in Arabic, but Lewis says the connection is purely accidental.

harandra (OSP)   High ground on *Malacandra. *Handra* in *Hrossan means land; prefix *har* means high in Old Norse, although Lewis suggests his use of *har* for mountain is accidental. Thus, *har* plus *(h)andra* creates *harandra*. Sorns dwell in caves on these *harandras*, where there is little oxygen and warmth because of the attack of the *Bent Oyarsa.

Hardcastle, Miss (THS)   "The Fairy." Homosexual head of *N.I.C.E.'s Institutional Police (*W.A.I.P.). Has been a suffragette, pacifist, British Fascist, imprisoned, and has met famous people. Big, thickly built; has square, stern, pale face with short iron-gray hair; deep voice; holds long rolled or chewed cheroot between her teeth. Killed by tiger let loose in the banquet hall. *Hard* fits with other *Belbury names. In "Reply to Professor *Haldane" *(Of Other Worlds)*, Lewis says Miss Hardcastle "is the common factor in all revolutions; and, as she says, you won't get anyone to do her job well unless they get some kick out of it."

Harry (OSP)   Idiot-boy who works for *Weston and *Devine at The *Rise and whom they first think of sending to *Mars. Harry's mother persuades *Ransom to find Harry and send him home.

Head (THS)   "Head" of *N.I.C.E. belonging to François *Alcasan, a convicted murderer. Lewis paints a disgusting picture of this green head with beard, nose, colored glasses, slobbering mouth, and endless tubes extending out of the top of its open skull. Alcasan, we learn, is not really alive, but his vocal organs and brain have become conductors for regular communication between the *Macrobes (evil eldila) and man. Charles Lindbergh was interested in achieving immortality for man by artificially perfusing a head severed from the body. He worked in the Department of Experimental Surgery of the Rockefeller Institute for Medical Research, collaborating with Alexis Carrel on constructing an apparatus that could pump synthetic blood through organs. Lewis also got the idea from Olaf *Stapledon's *Last and First Men* in which scientists try to construct a bodiless brain which will dominate them. Lewis recorded a dream in his diary (Sept. 12, 1923) about a scientist discovering how to keep the consciousness and motor nerves alive in a corpse, creating an immortal dead man. He also read by chance in the newspaper of a German experiment to keep a dog's head alive artificially.

Hegel, G. W. H. (THS)   (1770-1831) Philosopher read by *Wither who believed historical stages of philosophical ideas represented various stages in the development of the human spirit toward maturity.

Hingest, William (THS)   "Bill the Blizzard." *Bracton fellow and physical chemist of international reputation who tries to leave Belbury when he sees what it is like and is murdered. Family was of almost mythical antiquity, "never contaminated." Has old-fashioned curly white and yellow moustache, large beaklike nose, bald head. In a letter, Lewis says he is the only real distinguished and untainted scientist at *Belbury.

Hisperica Famina (THS)   Ancient Latin work famous for its extraordinary vocabulary. Divided into sections that describe a scene or object. *Merlin's speech is said to be as smooth as this work.

Hlab-Eribol-ef-Cordi (P)   Original speech of all the planets. Can be compared to the story of the Tower of Babel, before which all peoples of the earth spoke one language.

hluntheline (OSP)   (*see* **wondelone**) *Hrossan word for to long, crave for something wrongly, desire to possess the object, obtain it, receive pleasure from it rather than appreciate it for itself.

hnakra, hnéraki (OSP) Aquatic sea monster with snapping jaws who was born in the northern mountains of *Malacandra. Let in by *Maleldil, perhaps symbolic of the cold and evil caused by the Bent *Oyarsa of earth. Both the enemy and beloved of the *hrossa because it allows a sweet danger to be found in the woods. Poetic, has joy, roams; the spirit of the valley lies in him. Vulnerable in open mouth and killed by *Ransom and the hrossa. *Snakr* means snake in Old Norse and Icelandic; thus, it is the traditional symbol for evil.

hnau/nau (OSP)   Rational beings with spirit/soul (*Oyeresu, *eldila, men, *hrossa, *sorns, and *pfifltriggi). In a letter, Lewis says his source may be the Greek *nous* (spirit).

hross/hrossa (OSP) fem. pl. hressni   One of three intelligent creatures of Malacandra, reminiscent of seal, otter, and penguin. Thick black coat (also white), short legs with webbed feet, webbed claws; round, whiskered head; short tail. Six to seven feet high. Black and silver crested hrossa in west are ten feet high. Marry at 40, live 160 earth years, temperature 103°. Good at farming, fishing, poetry. Have stone-age culture, boil to cook, eat fish and vegetables. Sleep on the ground, live in villages in the *handramits* by the river in beehive-shaped huts made of stiff leaves. Language and lifestyle reminiscent of Old Norse. *Hross* means horse in Old Norse. Lewis says he got the word from the root of Wal*russ* (whale-horse), *ros*marine (in Spenser), and possibly *hors*hwael (horse-whale) in K. Aelfred's version of Orosius.

hru (OSP)   *Hrossan word for blood. *Arbol hru* is sun's blood, or gold. *Cru* means blood in Irish.

Hume, David (THS)   (1711-76) Philosopher read by *Wither. A Scottish skeptic who believed all our ideas come from sense impressions and therefore habit. Thus, knowledge cannot be certain. Extended these same ideas to ethics.

Humphrey (P)   Doctor called to be ready when *Ransom returns to earth in case he is injured on *Perelandra. Humphrey Carpenter says he is based on R. E. "Humphrey" Havard, Lewis's and Tolkien's physician and member of the Inklings.

Hutchinsons (THS)   Family which occupies ground floor apartment below the *Studdocks.

Inner Ring (THS)   Group or clique. A theme found throughout *THS* (Lewis says it is the main theme), but growing out of Lewis's own experience. His feelings about such groups can be found in his essay "The Inner Ring" published in *The Weight of Glory.*

Ironwood, Grace (THS)   Businesslike doctor for *Ransom at *St. Anne's. Dressed all in black, extremely tall, big, with large nose and lips, grey eyes; about 50. *Iron* and *wood* seem like a contradiction; *grace* significant.

Jewel, Canon (THS)   Canon of *Bracton College who tries to stop sale of *Bragdon Wood; of the "old school." Old, white-haired; childish face. In *English Literature in the Sixteenth Century,* Lewis mentions John Jewel (1522-71), who was famous for devotional writings and his speech attacking new rhetoric.

Joe (THS)   *Hardcastle's driver; car breaks down during arrest of Jane *Studdock.

Jules, Horace (THS)   Puppet director for *N.I.C.E. Scientific popularizer, editor of weekly *We Want to Know,* novelist. Attended University of London 50 years ago. Cockney, conceited, little; has short legs and turned up nose; "good liver." Shot by Fairy *Hardcastle at the banquet. Possibly a caricature of H. G. Wells (sounds like H. Jules). In a letter Lewis says he is "only a novelist."

Jupiter (THS)   *Glundandra, Glund, Glund-Oyarsa, Jove. Greatest planet, uninhabitable; confused with God; associated with kingship, power, stateliness, light, music, festal pomp, life and radiant health, dance, magnanimity, courtesy, laughter, solemnity, hugeness.

King, the (P)   Tor-Oyarsa, Oyarsa-Perelendri, *Tor, *Ask, *Baru, *Yatsur. Adam-figure. Learns strange things in *Lur (of evil, good, anguish, joy), while the *Green Lady is tempted. Described as God's live image and masterpiece.

Kitty (THS)   Member of the *W.A.I.P.

Klingsor (THS)   Jane *Studdock likens *St. Anne's garden to that of Klingsor, magician in version of the Grail legend adopted by Wagner in his opera *Parsifal.*

Laird, David (THS)   Politician and pragmatometrist who is to replace Mark *Studdock as *Bracton fellow. From Leicester, Cambridge. One of the most brilliant men in his class, president of the Sphinxes, editor of *The Audit. Laird* is a form of lord *(OED).*

Lancaster (THS)   Christian who left college after Mark *Studdock, considered dangerous by *N.I.C.E. Influential in Lower House of Convocation; mixed up with big clerical families; involved with Repton Conference; has written many books.

Lancelot (THS)   Most splendid and chivalrous of Arthurian knights, but lover of Guinevere and thus unable to attain full vision of the Grail. Beseiged by *Arthur in his castle after he saves Queen from burning at the stake. Withdraws to France and arrives home too late to help Arthur at Camlann. Dies in Glastonbury hermitage.

Layamon (THS)   (c. 1205) Wrote *Brut,* first Arthurian account in English.

Life-Force (P)   *Weston's "Spirit" toward which all the universe is moving. God and the Devil are both a portrait of it. In *Mere Christianity,* Lewis defined the Life-Force or creative/emergent evolution as the idea that life evolved not by chance, but by the "striving" or "purposiveness" of the Life-Force, a vague entity which is a type of tame, mindless god.

Lilith (THS)   According to Hebrew mythology, Adam's first wife, created before Eve, who refused to submit to Adam and became *Satan's dam. Jane *Studdock recalls a quote about Lilith, then sees the very book at *St. Anne's. Tied in with theme of obedience in marriage.

logical positivism (THS)   Philosophy once held by *Wither which says philosophy clarifies the meaning of statements, classifying them as either scientific, mathematical, or nonsensical.

Logres (THS)   Group at *St. Anne's representing a perfect order and civilization, a human political body in harmony with God's spiritual law and will. Opposite of Britain (the secular will of man, chaos). England sways between these two choices. Lewis's source

is Charles *Williams, whose Logres represents God's rule on
*earth. From Welsh *Lloegr,* a fairyland within Britain, or another
name for Britain itself. Called Loegria, Loengre in *History of the
Kings of England,* where it refers to the kingdom south of the Hum-
ber and east of the Severn, the land of the English invaders. Locryn
was Brutus' successor. Geoffrey of Monmouth derives the name
from the legendary King Locrine, who received it when Brutus divided Britain. The name is also found in Chretien of Troyes.

Lur (P, THS)   Green sea where forests grow up from the bottom
through the waves. *Lur* is the Assyrian word for fortress.

Lurga (THS)   (*see* **Saturn**)

Lyly (THS)   Christian who left Bracton after Mark *Studdock. On
a reactionary commission about education. *N.I.C.E. considers him
dangerous.

Lyndsay, Sir David (THS)   (1486-1555) Last of the major
medieval poets in England. Lewis got the title *That Hideous Strength*
from Lyndsay's description of the Tower of *Babel in *Ane Dialog
(The Monarche,* 1553): "The Shadow of that hyddeous strength sax
myle [six miles] and more it is of length."

MacPhee, Andrew (THS)   Skeptical, objective, logical Ulster
Scot who is a member of *St. Anne's and considered necessary to
the group. *Ransom's friend for years. Tall, grizzle-headed,
shrewd; hard-featured face. Wants fact, not opinion. Not permitted
to search for *Merlin because he is not a Christian and thus susceptible to evil. In a letter, Lewis says he is an "untainted and unspeci-
fied" scientist. Probably based on Lewis's objective tutor Kirkpat-
rick. MacPhee is a skeptical character in *The *Dark Tower.*

Macrobes (THS)   Bent/black *eldila; more intelligent than man.

Maenad (P)   Female member of the cult of Dionysus; frenzied,
"one who is mad." Lewis says the *Green Lady might dance like
one.

Malory, Sir Thomas   (1408-71) Author of *Le Morte d'Arthur,* one
of the most famous versions of the *Arthurian legend.

Maggs, Ivy (THS)   Jane *Studdock's maid, member of *St.
Anne's. *Ivy* suggests Nature and naturalness.

Maggs, Tom (THS)   Ivy's husband, in prison for petty theft (he stole money from the laundry he worked for); taken to *Belbury for rehabilitation. Married only six weeks. *Maggs* means to pilfer *(OED)*.

magic (THS)   According to Renaissance occultists, there were two kinds of magic: white *(magia)* and black *(goetia)*. Lewis says there was a time when white magic was possible, when there were neutral intelligences in earth. Now such magic as Merlin's is forbidden. He suggests there were three periods: the age before the "Great Disaster"; the Renaissance, when the soul went out of Nature; the 20th c.

Malacandra (OSP, P, THS)   (*see* **Mars**) *Ransom says this is the real, mythic name of Mars. An older, dying planet attacked by the *Bent One of earth. *Malac* is *hrossan for earth/planet; *(h)andra* means land. *Malan* means earth, soil in Gothic; *malac* is Hebrew for king; *malak* means messenger, angel, reign in Hebrew. Hooper and Green suggest *malo* in Latin, meaning "I would rather be, would to God that we were there," is appropriate.

Maleldil (OSP, P, THS)   Lewis says Maleldil is God the Father

Maleldil the Young (OSP)   Christ. In a letter, Lewis says Maleldil the Young is God the Son. He is presented as a slight change of light, feeling of well-being, sweet odors, heaviness in the knees. *Mal* seems to suggest "bad." But *Mal* in Gothic means king, and in Hebrew means a great heavenly being. *Malac* is Hebrew for king. In a letter, Lewis says he chose the name for its liquidity.

Mars (OSP, THS)   (*see* **Malacandra**) Also called Malacandra, Mavors, Marspiter, Tyr. Associated with war, iron, cold, clearness, the wolf.

Martha (THS)   The Dimbles' housekeeper.

McNeill, Janice (THS)   Daughter of headmaster of Campbell College, Belfast, and lifelong friend of Lewis. *THS* is dedicated to her.

McPhee (P)   Skeptical friend of *Ransom who argues against Christian doctrine of the resurrection. Probably the same as Mac-Phee in *THS*.

Melchisedec (THS)   In the Bible, "priest of the Most High God," "king of Salem," and ideal king of Israel, both priest and king (Gen. 14:18). Christ's priesthood is of the order of Melchisedec. Lewis says it is he "in whose hall the steep-stoned ring sparkles on the forefinger of the *Pendragon." *Arthur, *Enoch, *Elias, *Moses, and Melchisedec are said to dwell in *Abhalljin/Aphallin.

Meldilorn (OSP)   Island where the *Malacandrian *Oyarsa dwells. Island in circular sapphire lake with tall flowers like trees; pale, red, warm, soft, and fragrant.

Mercury (THS)   (*see* **Viritrilbia**) Also called Thoth, Viritrilbia. God of language; messenger. Associated with leaping, meaning, heart of language, source of words, quicksilver.

Merlin Ambrosius (THS)   High Council of *Logres (counsels the *Pendragon). In Lewis he is a gigantic 5th c. Druid, member of an ancient Celtic religious order, a Christian man and penitent. Buried but not dead for 1,500 years under *Bragdon Wood, he is reawakened so that his soul may be saved and so his mind can be used by the *Oyeresu. He is the last vestige of a special relationship with Nature that goes back to *Numinor. According to Nennius and Gildas, he is survivor of a noble Roman family who leads the Britons against the Anglo-Saxon invaders after withdrawal of Roman legions and who is also a wonder-worker. Geoffrey of Monmouth combined his miraculous exploits with those of the Welsh prophet Myrddin to produce Merlin, and also identified him with Ambrosius, a fatherless boy with second sight. Supposedly a child of Nimue and *Satan, although Lewis says his father need not have been bad. Charmed into a permanent state of enchantment. A wizard, Arthur's teacher in many legends. In a letter, Lewis says he, like everyone, did not know much about Merlin, so he had a free hand in portraying him. He recommends possible sources for information: Malory, E. K. Chamber's *Arthur of Britain,* Collingwood's *Oxford History of England* (Vol. 1), and Vinaver's Malory. Many feel he is also based on Yeats's Merlin.

Merlin's Well (THS)   Well under the center of *Bragdon Wood where *Merlin lies in enchantment for 1,500 years. A crypt, slab surrounded by stonework and Roman brick. An 800-yard tunnel leads outside to the south of the wood. Named Merlin's Well during Queen Elizabeth's reign, says Lewis, when Warden *Shovel surrounded the wood with a wall and named the well Merlin's. Bickering between troopers and the college in the heart of Bragdon occurred during the time of Cromwell; Richard *Crowe was killed on the steps of the well. Thus, every Warden of Bracton, on the day of his election, drinks a ceremonial cup of well water. Also the place where Sir Kenelm Digmby lay one night and saw strange appearances, and where Collins the poet had lain, George III cried, and Nathaniel Fox composed a poem. According to Clyde Kilby, Lewis told his friend George Sayer that he believed Merlin's Spring was actually located in the heart of the deer grove at Magdalen College. Many believe Bragdon Wood is based on the wood not far from Lewis's rooms; in a letter, Lewis remarks how Bragdon Wood is similar to the deer grove at Magdalen.

mice (THS) Mice eat the crumbs in *Ransom's room, illustrating obedience. In a letter Lewis wrote: "I love real mice. There are lots in my rooms in college, but I never set a trap." As he studied, they poked their heads out as if to say, "Time for *you* to go to bed. We want to come out and play."

Middle Earth (THS) Lewis probably derived this term from J. R. R. Tolkien. From *Middle erd* or *Midgard,* earth between Heaven and Hell—the center of the universe.

moon (OSP, THS) Sulva. Seen as the boundary (*Satan's shield) between earth and Deep Heaven. Because of Satan, all the space between earth and the moon is "under quarantine." This idea comes from a medieval tradition that the circle made by the orbit of the moon creates a boundary. In myth, the moon is called Artemis or Diana, the virgin and huntress. It is associated with silver (*Sulva* may thus be a sound-alike name). Also according to tradition, half of the moon was said to have life. *Filostrato believes intelligent life is found under the moon's surface; he praises the barren sterility of the side toward earth and says the far side has filthy organic life. *Ransom, on the other hand, says the side toward earth shares earth's curse, for the *Bent One smote it with his left hand and scarred it. It is barren, its marriages cold, while the other half looks toward Deep Heaven. On the cursed side dwell an accursed people, full of pride and lust. They do not lie together, but sleep with images of their mates, fabricating real children by "vile arts" in a secret place. Lewis is thus drawing on the "virgin" association of the moon and contrasting it with his *Venus (mother love) ideal as a theme of *THS*.

Mordred (THS) Illegitimate son and nephew of *Arthur by his half-sister *Morgawse. Traitor who usurps the throne, symbol of the corruption underlying Arthur's court. Arthur kills Mordred, but is wounded himself and carried to *Avalon.

Morgan (THS)   Morgan le Fay, *Arthur's half-sister and daughter of Ygerne by her first husband. Becomes a witch and troubles the kingdom with plots and magic.

Morgawse (THS)   *Arthur's half-sister, captured by Lot of Orkney, and becomes his queen and a spy in King Arthur's court. Unwittingly commits incest with Arthur and gives birth to *Mordred.

Morning Day (P)   Day on which the world is born and on which the King and Queen take over the throne of *Perelandra as Adam and Eve were meant to take over earth.

Morning Star (P)   Venus, promised to the *Green Lady and King. In "The Weight of Glory," Lewis says, "If we believe that God will one day *give* us the Morning Star and cause us to *put on* the splendour of the sun, then we may surmise that both the ancient myths and the modern poetry, so false as history, may be very near the truth as prophecy."

Moses (THS)   Said to dwell with *Enoch, *Elias, *Melchisedec, and *Arthur in *Abhalljin/Aphallin. Moses died, was buried by God, and was present with Jesus and Elijah at the transfiguration of Jesus (Matt. 17:3).

Much Nadderby (OSP)   Town where *Ransom is refused a room, forcing him on to The *Rise. Variation of adder or serpent *(OED)*.

Myrtle (THS)   Mark *Studdock's twin sister. He was greatly influenced by her and tried to be drawn into her circle of friends.

Natvilcius (P)   According to Lewis's footnote, author (fictitious) who describes eldilic creature in his work *De Aethereo at aerio Corpore* (Basel 1627) II, xii: "It appears that the homogeneous flame perceived by our senses is not the body, properly so called, of an angel or demon, but rather either the sensorium of that body or the surface of a body which exists after a manner beyond our conception in the celestial frame of special references." Natvilcius probably comes from Nat Whilk (Anglo-Saxon for "I know not whom"), Lewis's pen name for his poems.

Neruval (P)   The iron plain of Neruval is mentioned in *Perelandra,* but we are not told whether Neruval is another planet, such as Uranus, Neptune, or Pluto. It could also be a plain on *Mars (associated with iron).

N.I.C.E. (THS)   The National Institute of Co-ordinated Experiments with headquarters at *Belbury. Its goals are fusion of state and applied scientific research; control of environment and man's destiny; selective breeding; freeing man from body, birth, breeding, death, the organic, and the subjective; remedial treatment of criminals; placing Man Immortal on the throne of the universe using Nature as instrument. Its symbol is a nude male with thunderbolt (*see* **Zeus**). Under control of the *Dark Eldila. Although obvious sarcasm is found in the word *nice,* actually the word *nice* is derived from Latin *nescius* (ignorant) and an Old French word for silly, and means foolish, wanton, stupid, senseless in Middle English. Jane *Studdock wants to "be with Nice people, away from Nasty people."

Nimrod (THS)   In Gen. 10:8, 9, son of Cush and founder of Babylon; a mighty hunter. In Sir David Lyndsay's *The Monarche,* described as being huge of stature. Became king, proposed building Tower of Babel, and introduced idolatry.

Non-Olet (THS)   (*see* **Place, Charles**) N.O. or Charles Place, elderly warden of *Bracton. Nicknamed N.O. by those against the *Progressive Element (die-hards) and was a disappointment. From the Latin phrase "non-olet" meaning, "it does not stink," said of money from questionable sources.

Northumberland (THS)   College opposite *Bracton on the River Wynd, where *Dimble teaches. In a letter Lewis says Northumberland is a glorious word and exemplifies his love of syllables.

Numinor (THS)   True, utter West; Atlantis; Eden. Fallen land beyond the sea. Was in its prime in preglacial days when Nature and spirit were more unified and thus magic could be an art, and when man was closer to the gods. Lewis says it is his misspelling of Tolkien's Numenor. Tolkien said Lewis misspelled the word since he never saw the word written and was probably influenced by *numinous.* From *numen,* meaning divinity *(OED).*

Objective Room (THS)   Room at *Belbury designed to kill all human reactions and promote objectivity. Ill-proportioned, with lopsided door, spots on ceiling and table, and surreal pictures.

O'Hara, Captain (THS)   Second in command of *N.I.C.E. police. Big, white-haired man with handsome face; of ancient family; has Scottish or Irish accent and a seat at Castlemortle.

Old One (OSP)   (*see* **Maleldil**) God.

Ouroborindra (THS)   Word uttered by *Straik, *Filostrato, and *Wither as they worship the *Head during the final moments of *Belbury. *Uroboros* in Greek means one that devours its tail. The Serpent that devours its own tail is a creature found in Norse cosmology. It circles the earth (called the Midgardsorm) and is to be earth's downfall at the twilight of the gods by devouring it.

Oyarsa/Oyéresu   (also Oyarses, Ousiarches, Oeyarsu) (*see* **Bernardus Silvestris**) Greatest of *eldila, the planetary intelligences who rule each planet; every planet has an Oyarsa. All Oyeresu communicate with each other; however, earth's Oyarsa (*Satan) has become bent, so earth is silent. Pure spiritual, intellectual love; does not die, breed, breathe; body hard to see. The Oyeresu of *Mars and *Venus appear to *Ransom in various forms similar to Ezekiel's description in the Bible: flames, eyes, and wheels. Ransom describes the Oyarsa of *Malacandra as a silence in a crowded room, memory of forgotten sound and scent, that which is smallest, stillest, and hardest to seize in Nature. According to Bernardus Silvestris, Lewis's source, an Oyarsa is the deputed power of each planet, the "genius" to whom God has given power over natural things and who gives shape to the forms of things. In the last chapter of *OSP*, Lewis says it is not accidental that Silvestris uses this word because the 12th c. is in the same celestial year as earth in Lewis's day. Hooper and Green believe the source for the Oyeresu and eldila may have been Lewis's idea for a poem about Simon Magus, a gnostic magician who takes Helen to *Zeus and fights "the Dynasties" or planets on the way.

Oyarsa-Perelendri (P)   *Tor and *Tinidril are called the Oyarsa-Perelendri by the former *Oyarsa of *Perelandra, signifying that they are now the rulers of the planet and he has given his charge over to them.

Pamela (THS)   Childhood friend of Myrtle, Mark *Studdock's twin sister, and member of her *"Inner Ring."

Paracelsus (THS)   Swiss alchemist, Lewis's example of "occult" magician. In *The Abolition of Man,* Lewis says the characters of magician and scientist are combined in Paracelsus.

"Paradise Lost"   Milton's epic story of Adam and Eve. Lewis's key analysis of this poem, *Preface to Paradise Lost,* was published in 1941, a year before *Perelandra* was completed, and his interpretation of Milton's poem greatly influenced his own portrayal of the fall in *Perelandra.* Although many aspects of the temptation scenes in *Paradise Lost* and *Perelandra* are comparable, Lewis introduces a new "Adam" and "Eve," *eldila, a human agent to help the *Green Lady, a human "serpent," the *Fixed Land as the command, and a happy and victorious ending.

Pearson (THS)   Mark *Studdock's former childhood friend.

Pelham (THS)   *Bracton fellow, considered to be an "unfortunate choice." Has a buttonlike mouth and "pudding face."

Pendragon (THS)   British or Welsh prince claiming supreme power; King of Britain, father of *Arthur, called Uther by Malory. King of *Logres, descendant of Arthur, as ruler of the ideal kingdom. *Pendragon* is the Welsh word for dragonhead; the king had a dragonhead standard. Lewis says there was an unbroken succession of Pendragons from Arthur on, related to the *Plantagenets, and the title was handed down from generation to generation. *Ransom is the 79th Pendragon and will pass on the title when he returns to *Perelandra at the close of *THS.* The Pendragons of England are said to give the "push" or "pull" to prod England out of the final outrage into which Britain has tempted her.

Perelandra (P)   (*see* **Venus**) The planet, the god herself who comes for *Ransom, the goddess of love, and the earthly wraith of Venus who has mistakenly been identified as Greek and Roman goddess Ishtar or Aphrodite. This wraith appears to Jane *Studdock as a giant in a flame-colored robe with exposed breasts, honey-colored skin; black eyes, red cheeks, wet lips; she causes ivy, honeysuckle, and lilies to grow over everything in the lodge. The planet is a unique and perfect world, younger than earth, with gold sky and waves, floating islands, and a dense atmosphere. *Per* means perfect in Latin. *Peril* suggests the "almost Fall." Lewis spells it "Parelandra" in *OSP,* suggesting "paradise"; Hooper and Green suggest "fairy land."

pfifltrigg/pfifltriggi (OSP)   One of the three *hnau of *Malacandra. Like reptile, grasshopper, and frog. Small, hairless, tapir-headed; long in snout; pale. Has long, pointed yellow forehead, many fingers; makes dry, raspy sound when it moves and has a piping laugh. Oviparous, matriarchal, short-lived. Pfifltriggi live in houses with pillars in the forests and mines on Malacandra's old ocean beds. Are diggers, singers, and craftsmen who make both aesthetic and useful objects. In a letter, Lewis says one can pronounce the *pf* in the name like the German *pferd*.

philologist (OSP)   One who studies language. Since *Ransom is a philologist, he becomes immediately interested in *Malacandrian language and wants to write a dictionary. In a letter, Lewis says he made Ransom a philologist chiefly to render his mastery of *Old Solar more plausible. Lewis's friend J. R. R. Tolkien was a philologist, and Lewis himself was a student of many languages.

Piebald (P)   Perelandrian creatures that are like mice, yet reminiscent of sheep having larger ears, mobile noses, longer tails, and are white and fluffy with black spots. The *Green Lady nicknames *Ransom Piebald because he is red from the sun on one side of his body, but white on the side that was in shadow during his space journey. *Piebald* means two different colors (white and dark) in irregular patches; motley *(OED)*.

Pinch (THS)   Cat at *St. Anne's. Has a special relationship with Mr. *Bultitude, illustrating, says *Ransom, one of *Barfield's "ancient unities."

Place, Charles (THS)   (*see* **Non-Olet**) Nicknamed N.O./Non-Olet. Warden of *Bracton College, elected 15 years ago by the *Progressive Element and arrested by *N.I.C.E. Elderly civil servant, had been in an obscure Cambridge College; wrote a monumental report on national sanitation. Is a dyspeptic, is "seldom heard," and has a taste for philately.

Plantagenets (THS)   Lewis says the *Pendragons from *Arthur on were related to the Plantagenets. This was an English royal house of 14 kings who reigned from 1154 to 1485, including Henry II, Richard I, John, Henry III, Edward I, II, III, Richard II, Henry IV, V, VI, Edward IV, V, and Richard III.

pragmatism (THS)   Philosophy once held by *Wither which is a method of solving problems by analyzing a theory on the basis of whether it "works." If it does, it is **true**.

pragmatometer (THS)   Gadget at *Belbury which prints the findings of the Committee on the Analytical Notice-Board every half hour.

Prescott, Mary (THS)   *Edgestow resident who is raped and battered during *N.I.C.E. instigated riots.

Progressive Element (THS)   *Inner Ring of *Bracton College, including *Curry, *Busby, and *Feverstone. Opponents called "obstructionists." Believe the college needs "new blood" and to be shaken out of its "academic grooves." Want sale of *Bragdon Wood to *Belbury.

Prospero (THS)   Shakespeare's Duke of Milan, a magician. Lewis's example of a ceremonial scientist and magician.

Psalms of the Eldila (P)   Source for Lewis's worshipful psalms at the end of *Perelandra* may be the *Mishnah,* part of the Hebrew Talmud, which is similar in structure, tone, and theme:

Therefore but a single man was created in the world, to teach that if any man has caused a single soul to perish, Scripture imputes it to him as though he had caused the whole world to perish; and if any man saves alive a single soul, Scripture imputes it to him as though he had saved alive a whole world. . . . Again (but a single man was created) to proclaim the greatness of the Holy One, Blessed be He; for a man stamps many coins with the one seal and they are all alike one another; but the King of Kings, the Holy One, blessed is He, has stamped every man with the seal of the first man, and yet not one of them is like his fellow. Therefore everyone must say, For my sake the world was created.

Ransom, Elwin (OSP, P, THS)   (*see* **Elwin**) In the Postscript of *OSP,* Lewis says Dr. Ransom is only a fictitious name for his Cambridge friend who really went to *Mars. *Philologist, fellow of Cambridge College, don, Christian, around 40 or 50 years old; has a married sister in India. Like Lewis, he is a walker, good swimmer, "sedentary scholar," bachelor, antivivisectionist, has war wound. Wrote *Dialect and Semantics.* In a letter, Lewis says he made Ransom a philologist chiefly to render his mastery of *Old Solar more plausible. Becomes *Pendragon of *Logres and the *Fisher-King. Ransom says his name comes from "Ranolf's son," but learns that he is not named Ransom for nothing: it is the "name of a payment that delivers," and a Voice (Christ) tells him, "My name also is Ransom." Lewis says that Ransom is "a *figura Christi,*" or Christ-figure, only in the sense that every Christian should be and is called upon to enact Christ. Humphrey Carpenter feels that Ransom is also a portrait of J. R. R. Tolkien (philologist, has same opinions) and Charles *Williams (spiritual strength, quiet, and vigor).

Raynor (THS)   *Bracton fellow.

Rhodes, Cecil (THS)   (1853-1902) British financier and colonist.

Rise, The (OSP)   House where *Devine and *Weston work and construct their spaceship.

Rowley (THS)   Man arrested by *N.I.C.E.

Rumbold (THS)   Solicitor; Mark *Studdock hears gossip about him in Courthampton.

Sancho (THS)   *Bracton fellow.

Sandown (THS)   Wooded and hilly area northwest of *Edgestow where Mark and Jane *Studdock live and where Jane picnics with the *Dennistons.

Satan (P)   (see **Bent One**) Also called the *Black Archon, Bent *Oyarsa, Evil One, Bent One. The Bent Oyarsa is said to be brighter and greater than *Malacandra's Oyarsa, just as Lucifer was greatest of angels and is called the "Shining One" and "bearer of Light" (also see Isa. 14:12-14). Lewis portrays him, as he is in the Bible, as "ruler of this world" (John 12:31; 16:11) and "god of this world" (2 Cor. 4:4). Ransom says the *Un-man is unlike Mephistopheles or Satan in *Paradise Lost because they are too grand and heroic, not contemptible.

Saturn (THS)   Lurga. Associated with cold, numbing weight and pressure, and antiquity. In astrology, characterized by remoteness and slowness; lead; is supposed to cause coldness and sluggishness.

Schiaparelli, Giovanni (P)   In 1877 discovered "canals" (really grooves) on *Mars. Lewis mentions his theory that *Perelandra revolves once on herself in the same time it takes to go around the sun, thus creating perpetual day on one side, perpetual night on the other. *Ransom proves him wrong.

scientism   An outlook on the world connected with the popularization of the sciences—e.g., belief in perpetuation of the species. Not to be confused with science.

Seven Bears of Logres (THS)   Mr. *Bultitude is said to be last of the Seven Bears of Logres. In a letter, Lewis says this and the *Atlantean Circle were pure invention, made up on analogy with the Nine Worthies or Celtic Triads.

shooter (THS)   Any college servant at *Bracton.

Shovel (THS)   Warden of *Bracton during Queen Elizabeth's reign who named the crypt under *Bragdon Wood *"Merlin's Well."

Sid (and Len) (THS)   Truck drivers for *N.I.C.E. who steal Mr. *Bultitude. Sid wants "out" of *Belbury.

Silent Planet (OSP)   (*see* **earth**)   Earth, *Thulcandra (*thulc* means silent in *hrossan). All planets speak the same language except earth, which has been cut off from communication with the rest of the planets because of its *Bent Oyarsa. Lewis may also be basing his idea on a medieval source. *Survival of the Pagan Gods,* a book which Lewis quotes in *The Discarded Image,* describes a medieval diagram which showed eight planets, with a muse corresponding to each. Earth's muse was called Thalia. The model contained eight celestial spheres, eight strings, eight musical modes, and eight muses, but earth made nine, one too many, thus destroying the perfection of the scheme. So Gafurio corrected this inconsistency by saying that earth, being motionless, was therefore silent.

Silvestris (OSP)   (*see* **Bernardus Silvestris**)

singing beast (P)   Most glorious, delicate, and wondrous of all beasts. Sings beautiful song of joy in a low, rich, full, passionate voice. Heard by *Ransom when he emerges from the cavern of *Perelandra. Size of a small elephant, with horse's neck; is black; has long bushy tail, round white belly; sits up like a dog; is very shy. Suckled by she-beast of another kind. Apprently it is higher in the hierarchy than other Perelandrian animals since in the final ceremony the four singing beasts come after Ransom and before the other animals. Reminiscent of the four creatures described by Ezekiel that are similar to the seraphim, whose duty it is to give glory and praise to God. Also similar to some of the creatures found in medieval bestiaries. Included in Jorge Luis Borges's *The Book of Imaginary Beings* as a beast totally made-up by Lewis.

sorn/séroni (OSP)   One of three *hnau of *Malacandra. The "intelligentsia," interested in factual information. About 18 feet tall, white; thin, spidery, and elongated; have narrow, conical heads and solemn, thin, long faces with small eyes and drooping noses and mouths; pouted chests; thin hands like a bird's; are covered with almost transparent feathers. *Sorn* means to sponge upon, depend on others for a living *(OED)*.

Soroborn (OSP)   Red *sorn of the northern desert of *Malacandra.

St. Anne's (THS)   Headquarters of *Logres, headed by *Ransom. Members include Ivy *Maggs, Cecil and Margaret *Dimble, Arthur and Camilla *Denniston, *MacPhee, and Jane *Studdock, plus a menagerie of animals. When Ransom's sister died, she told him a great danger was hanging over the human race. He was also told a company would collect around him, over which he would be Head. From Charles *Williams, Lewis got this idea of the "company," an overflow into Logres of the life lived in Taliessin, the poet's own house. In a letter, Lewis says he chose the name St. Anne's "merely as a plausible and euphonious name."

Stapledon, Olaf (OSP)   Lewis read Stapledon's *Last and First Men* (1930), in which scientists try to construct a bodiless brain which will dominate them, and wanted to replace this idea with a Christian point of view. Stapledon believed in an immaterial *Life-Force which shaped the universe and that man is in a state of evolution and must improve his power. Lewis also got the idea of *floating islands in *Perelandra* from this book.

Steele (THS)   H.D. (Head Director) for sociology at *N.I.C.E. Tall, unsmiling man with a long, horselike face and thick, pouting lips. Objects to Mark *Studdock. Killed by an elephant. Steele fits in with the hard coldness of other *Belbury names.

Sterk (OSP, THS)   Town outside *Edgestow where *Ransom hopes to find a hotel after his failure in *Much Nadderby. *Sterk* is obsolete form of stark *(OED)*.

Stock (THS)   *N.I.C.E. nutritionist.

Stoke Underwood (OSP)   Town where *Ransom spends the night on his walking tour. *Stoke* is a common place name.

Stone (THS)   *Belbury employee who seems to be in trouble with *N.I.C.E. Mark *Studdock first meets him in *Wither's office and tries to talk to him later. Searches for *Merlin. *Stone* fits in with the other Belbury names.

Storey, Canon (THS)   Leads funeral for *Hingest; isolated from others by his faith and deafness.

Strabo (THS)   Author of *Balachthon*. Greek geographer who wrote a geographical work describing the various continents.

Straik, Reverend (THS)   Mad Welsh parson of *N.I.C.E. Believes science is the instrument of God toward a kingdom on earth. Undergoes brainwashing like Mark *Studdock. Has dark, lean, tragic face; wears threadbare clothes, clumsy boots, frayed clerical collar; does not drink or smoke. *Wither slashes him with a knife in the laboratory. *Straik* is a type of measure *(OED)*.

Strand, The (THS)   Periodical in which Mark *Studdock reads a story he had started as a child. Popular illustrated monthly magazine like *Harper's*. Began in England in 1891; the American edition (1891-1916) had English content—stories such as "Country of the Blind" by H. G. Wells.

Studdock, Jane Tudor (THS)   Twenty-three-year-old wife of Mark, working on her doctorate on Donne's vindication of the body and thus is delaying having children. But she has lost interest in scholarship. Married for just six months, but sees it as solitary confinement and refuses obedience. Abandoned Christianity in early childhood, along with belief in fairies and Santa Claus. Does not want to commit herself or become involved. Valuable to *St. Anne's and *Belbury because of her visionary dreams; her ancestor was also a visionary. Likes severe clothes, dislikes femininity and sentimentality, but is attractive. Had potential of bearing future *Pendragon of *Logres. Her road to Christianity parallels Mark's throughout *THS;* her "conversion" is similar to Lewis's. Mrs. Moore, Lewis's "adopted mother," was named Jane. Also, *THS* is dedicated to Jane McNeill. Could be drawn from Lewis's own female pupils and members of the Socratic Club.

Studdock, Mark Gainsby (THS)   Sociologist, junior fellow of *Bracton College for five years. Attended Duke's College. Materialist, does not believe in God, has wrong commitment to *Inner Rings; likes to be liked (the "spaniel" in him). "Different men" in him appear rapidly until he "becomes a person" at the end of *THS*.

Sulva (THS)   (*see* **moon**) The moon. Has a secret evil, is shield of the Dark Lord (*Bent One), who scarred it by blows. In myth, the moon was associated with silver (sound-alike of *sulva*).

Sura (THS)   Native Christian mystic who was friend of *Ransom's sister in India. Said danger was hanging over human race; later disappeared. *Sura* in Hindu demonology is a good angel or genie.

Surnibur (OSP)   *Sorn speech.

Tai Harendrimar (P)   Hill of Life, the throne from which the King and Queen of *Perelandra reign. *Tai* in Welsh means house, mansion.

Taliessin Through Logres (THS)   Charles *Williams's poem of the Arthurian legend which greatly influenced many of Lewis's Arthurian ideas in *THS*. Lewis analyzes this poem in "Williams and the Arthuriad," which appears in *Taliessin Through Logres and the Region of the Summer Stars* and *Arthurian Torso*. Camilla *Denniston reads this poem.

Taylor (THS)   Mark *Studdock's former undergraduate friend.

Ted (THS)   *Bracton fellow.

Telford (THS)   *Bracton fellow.

Tellus (THS)   (*see* **earth**). Latin word for earth. In Roman myth, the planet earth and goddess of earth.

"That Hideous Strength" (THS)   This title comes from David Lyndsay's *Ane Dialog,* a description of the Tower of *Babel: "The Shadow of that hyddeous strength sax myle [six miles] and more it is of length." The Avon and Pan abridged version of THS was retitled *The Tortured Planet.*

Third Heaven (THS)   *Venus, the third planet created after *Mars and *earth; third unfallen planet from the sun. Name found in Charles *Williams's writings, referring to the sphere of Venus or Divine Love, "feeling intellect." In the Bible, refers to the abode of God, where Christ came from and ascended to and where the saints go upon death (2 Cor. 12:2).

Third One (THS)   The Holy Spirit. In a letter, Lewis says *Maleldil lives with the Old One, and these are God the Son and God the Father. The Third One, we are told, dwells with them.

Thulcandra (OSP) (*see* **earth, Tellus, Silent Planet**). Earth. From *hrossan *thulc* (silent) and *(h)andra* (earth, land). Lewis says Thulcandra is a portmanteau word from *thick, dull, sulk.*

Tinidril (P) *Green Lady, the Mother. *Tor, Tinidril, *Yatsurah seem to be from Hebrew verbs meaning to form.

Tor (P) King of Perelandra. The Anglo-Saxon word *tor* means rock or tower; may also come from Hebrew verb meaning to form. Tolkien felt Tor and Tinidril may echo his Tuor and Idril in "The Fall of Gondolin," blended with Tinuviel (second name of Luthien).

Un-man (P) Demon-possessed *Weston; *Satan's representative on *Perelandra. Looks like Weston, but the *Bent One is only using his body. Lewis's attempt to present the real picture of evil: as an imbecilic, apelike, nasty child with infantile laugh and performing petty obscenities. Destroyed in subterranean fire.

Urendi Maleldil (THS) Blessing used by *Ransom.

Uther (THS) (*see* **Pendragon**)

Venus (P, THS) (*see* **Perelandra**) The planet, the real goddess who takes *Ransom back to Perelandra, and the earthly wraith who appears to Jane *Studdock. Associated with mother, love, charity, fragrance, burning, beauty, vibration. In a flash makes visible the ultimate femininity of the universe. Lewis says the Renaissance Platonists saw Venus (celestial love and beauty) as a model after which the material universe was created. He also says Venus is a female deity, not because men invented the mythology, but because she is.

Viritrilbia (THS) (*see* **Mercury**) Mercury. In a letter, Lewis says he chose this word for its vibrating, tintillating quality befitting the subtlety of Mercury. Merlin refers to the earthly wraith Mercurius, who has been mistakenly deified as a Greek and Roman god.

vivisection (THS) Experimentation on living creatures in order to demonstrate already known facts or investigate new theory. Can include cutting, burning, freezing, deliberate infliction of disease. Practiced by *N.I.C.E. Lewis was opposed to vivisection and wrote a booklet for the National Anti-Vivisection Society of London. His essay "Vivisection" is published in *God in the Dock.*

Waddington, C. H. (THS) Eminent Cambridge embryologist and author of *Science and Ethics*. His theory of existence as its own justification is mentioned in *THS*. Also mentioned in lengthy footnote in *The Abolition of Man* as an example of one who tries to base value on fact. He says, "An existence which is essentially evolutionary is itself the justification for an evolution towards a more comprehensive existence." Lewis objects that, first, praising evolution on the basis of its properties is using an external standard, thus contradicting attempts to make existence its own justification. Second, he is not observing Nature as a whole in which life is working toward extinction, not improvement. In "Reply to Professor *Haldane" (*Of Other Worlds*), Lewis says *Frost is the mouthpiece of Waddington's ethical theories.

Wadsden (THS)   Mark *Studdock's former undergraduate friend.

W.A.I.P. (THS)   Women's Auxiliary Institutional Police at *Belbury, including Dolly, Daisy, and Kitty. All the girls except Fairy *Hardcastle, their Chief, are described as feminine, small, slight, fluffy, and full of giggles. In "Reply to Professor *Haldane," Lewis says, "The worst of all public dangers is the committee of public safety," which consists of men with a passion for power.

Wantage (P)   *Perelandra* is dedicated to "Some Ladies at Wantage." Lewis was friends with and corresponded with Sister Penelope of the Community of St. Mary the Virgin, an order of Anglican nuns in Wantage, Berkshire. Lewis was asked to conduct a conference for the convent. The translator of the Portuguese version of *Perelandra* mistranslated the phrase as "To some Wanton ladies"!

wardrobe (THS)   Large room which takes up major part of top floor of one wing at *St. Anne's.

water-people (P)   Mermaidlike inhabitants of *Perelandra, "Myth come alive" for Ransom. Reminiscent of the water creatures Lucy sees in *Voyage of the Dawn Treader*.

Watson (THS)   *Bracton fellow.

Wedenshaw (OSP)   *Ransom's and *Devine's school.

Weston, Edward Rolles (OSP, P)   (1896-1942). Lewis says this is his fictitious name. Great physicist who discovered Weston rays. Wants race to live forever and conquer other worlds. Demonized by *Bent Oyarsa on *Perelandra, where his philosophy has changed to emergent evolution, the belief that everything is moving toward Spirit or *Life-Force. *Ransom honors him by writing plaque for Weston on Perelandra. *N.I.C.E. says he was on their side and was murdered. Lewis says he believed the dangers of Westonism to be real. Some feel Weston was inspired by J. B. S. *Haldane. Name from "West on" or "Western." There was a real Edward Weston (1850-1936), an American electrical scientist and inventor.

W. H. Lewis (dedication of OSP)   Lewis's brother Warren.

Whin (OSP)   *Hross who hunts *hnakra with Hyoi and *Ransom. *Whin* is a type of grass *(OED)*.

Wilkins (THS)   *Filostrato's senior assistant.

Williams, Charles   Friend of Lewis and member of the Inklings. Lewis's source for much of his *Arthurian material comes from Williams's Arthurian poem *Taliessin Through Logres,* which he read to Lewis. Lewis wrote a critical study of this complex poem. Lewis got his idea of *Logres, white and black *magic, "the company" from Williams.

Winter, Mr. (THS)   *N.I.C.E. member. *Winter* fits in with other *Belbury names.

Wither, John (THS)   Deputy Director of *N.I.C.E. who has been taken over by evil *eldila. Old; has white, curly hair, a large face; watery, pouchy eyes; mask of skin and flesh; is very tall. Has a courtly manner and vague, noncommittal expression—"making things clear" is the one thing he can't stand. There is something vague and chaotic about his face and he never looks at you, but is excessively polite. Always whistles a dreary tune. Has ceased to believe in knowledge itself. Passed from *Hegel to *Hume to *pragmatism, then *logical positivism, and finally the void. His "ghost" or image appears frequently around *Belbury. Killed in lab by a bear. *Wither* is an appropriate name for the withered self he has become under the influence of the evil *eldila.

wondelone (OSP)   *(see* **hluntheline**) *Hrossan word for to long for. This is what Lewis called *Sehnsucht,* desire for joy. Longing for something without wishing to reexperience it except in memory and without desiring to possess the object.

Worchester (P)   Town where *Ransom's cottage is located. A real town of Worcester is located just north of Malvern, England, where Lewis went to school.

wound in heel (P, THS)   *Ransom acquires a wound in his heel from the bite of the Un-man which is always bleeding and can only be healed when he returns to *Perelandra. The wound has several meanings: (1) It is a symbol of the wound of Christ, just as Ransom is a figure of Christ; (2) It is a symbol for fallen humanity; (3) It is a symbol for man's mortality; (4) In myth, the *Fisher-King receives a "dolorous blow" from Balin the Savage (usually in his thigh) and thus the land is Waste. The wound is usually interpreted to be the result of sin.

Wrench, Inspector (THS)   *N.I.C.E. member who helps search for *Merlin. *Wrench* fits in with other *Belbury names.

Yatsur (P)   (*see* **Yatsurah**) King of *Perelandra.

Yatsurah (P)   Queen of *Perelandra, the *Green Lady. *Yatsurah* is probably derived from the Hebrew verbs meaning to form.

Zeus   Jupiter, king of the gods in mythology. Often portrayed as holding a thunderbolt. The symbol for *N.I.C.E. is a nude male holding a thunderbolt, representing man as king of the universe.

NOTES

All unpublished material is located in Marion Wade Collection, Wheaton College, Wheaton, Illinois.

All quotations at beginnings of chapters and appendixes are from *Perelandra*.

Quotations and sources used in the text are identified here by the page on which they appear and by the first few words quoted. Material in the Dictionary of Deep Heaven which is derived from outside sources is identified by the entry (printed in **bold type**).

page 11	"God will . . ." *Mere Christianity* (N.Y.: Macmillan, 1943), p. 66.
page 13	"The idea . . ." *Surprised by Joy* (N.Y.: Harcourt, Brace, & World, 1955), pp. 35, 36.
page 14	"He confessed . . ." "Unreal Estates," *Of Other Worlds* (N.Y. and London: Harcourt, Brace, Jovanovich, 1966), p. 87.
	"But he did . . ." "A Reply to Professor Haldane," *Ibid.*, p. 76.
page 15	"Like his friend . . ." *Letters of C. S. Lewis*, ed. W. H. Lewis (N.Y.: Harcourt, Brace, & World, 1966), pp. 278, 279.
page 16	"At the same . . ." Unpublished letter, December 11, 1940.
	"Still, he believed . . ." "Unreal Estates," *Of Other Worlds*, p. 89.
	"Those who . . ." H. G. Wells, *War of the Worlds* (1898; rpt. N.Y.: Berkley Medallion, 1964), pp. 21, 22.
	"Lewis believed . . ." "The Seeing Eye," *Christian Reflections* (Grand Rapids: Eerdmans, 1967), pp. 173, 174.
	"Lewis felt he was . . ." *Letters*, p. 295.

page 17   "He also classified . . ." See "On Science Fiction," *Of Other Worlds*.

"Such a work . . ." Roger Lancelyn Green and Walter Hooper, *C. S. Lewis: A Biography* (N.Y. and London: Harcourt, Brace, Jovanovich, 1974), p. 163.

"Although he liked . . ." Unpublished letter to Mr. Evans, February 28, 1949.

"The author would be . . ." Note to *Out of the Silent Planet*.

page 18   "What immediately . . ." Hooper and Green, *C. S. Lewis: A Biography*, p. 163.

page 19   "There is . . ." *Possible Worlds* (Harper and Bros., 1928), p. 305.

"To construct . . ." "On Stories," *Of Other Worlds*, p. 12.

"Lewis preferred . . ." Unpublished letter to Ruth Pitter, January 4, 1947.

"The 'real father' . . ." *Letters*, p. 205.

page 20   "His Tormance . . ." "On Stories," *Of Other Worlds*, p. 12.

"Other influences . . ." *Letters*, p. 205.

"A further . . ." *Letters*, pp. 166, 167.

"In fact . . ." Unpublished letter, June 1937.

"I begin to . . ." *Letters*, p. 210.

"In his . . ." "A Reply to Professor Haldane," *Of Other Worlds*, p. 76.

"Although the book . . ." *Letters*, p. 295.

"Afterwards, Lewis said . . ." *Letters*, p. 261.

page 21   "Lewis said . . ." *Letters*, p. 166.

page 22   "Actually, Lewis . . ." "It All Began With a Picture," *Of Other Worlds*, p. 42.

"Next, said . . ." "Unreal Estates," *Of Other Worlds*, p. 87.

page 23   "Suppose, even . . ." *Letters*, p. 283.

"By November . . ." *Letters*, pp. 195, 200.

"As with . . ." Unpublished letter to James Como, February 7, 1968.

"While Lewis . . ." Walter Hooper, "Preface," *Christian Reflections*, p. viii and unpublished letter to Martin, April 24, 1958.

"He reportedly . . ." Hooper and Green, *C. S. Lewis: A Biography*, p. 171.

"The Green . . ." *Letters*, p. 195.

page 24   "The book sold . . ." *Letters*, p. 209.

"In response . . ." W. H. Lewis, *C. S. Lewis: A Biography* (unpublished), letter to Ms. Vera Matthews, April 9, 1949, p. 323.

"Lewis calls . . ." Preface to *That Hideous Strength*.

"When asked . . ." Unpublished letter to Mr. Kinter, February 14, 1951.

"Lewis says . . ." Preface to *That Hideous Strength*.

"In *Of* . . ." "A Reply to Professor Haldane," *Of Other Worlds*, pp. 78-80.

page 25   "Finally, for . . ." Hooper and Green, *C. S. Lewis: A Biography*, pp. 174, 175.

page 28   "In 'The . . ." "The Seeing Eye," *Christian Reflections*, pp. 174, 176.
          "Lewis says this . . ." "A Reply to Professor Haldane," *Of Other Worlds*, p. 78.
page 30   "In *Mere* . . ." *Mere Christianity*, p. 51.
page 31   "Lewis says when . . ." "On Science Fiction," *Of Other Worlds*, p. 69.
page 34   "Lewis felt . . ." Unpublished letter to Martin, July 10, 1957.
          "Lewis says his . . ." W. H. Lewis, *C. S. Lewis: A Biography* (unpublished), letters to Charles Moorman, June 12, 1957, p. 414.

page 43   "All this time . . ." *The Discarded Image* (N.Y. and London: Cambridge U. Press, 1964), p. 116.
page 44   "He has a sense . . ." *The Great Divorce* (N.Y.: Macmillan, 1946), p. 27.
          "In modern . . ." *The Discarded Image*, pp. 74, 75.
          "God is the source . . ." *Miracles* (N.Y.: Macmillan, 1947), p. 90.
page 45   "But in *The* . . ." *The Problem of Pain* (1940; rpt. N.Y.: Macmillan, 1971), p. 127.
page 47   "Thus the men . . ." *The Discarded Image*, p. 116.
page 49   "Lewis writes . . ." *The Problem of Pain*, p. 150.
page 50   "In *Mere* . . ." *Mere Christianity*, p. 153.
page 52   "So, Medieval . . ." "Imagination and Thought in the Middle Ages," *Studies in Medieval and Renaissance Literature* (London: Cambridge U. Press, 1966), p. 54.
          "Lewis said . . ." Unpublished letter, April 29, 1943.
          "His eldila . . ." Unpublished letter to Martin, July 10, 1957.
page 54   "For if . . ." *Miracles*, p. 95.
          "Bernardus . . ." Bernardus Silvestris, *Cosmographia*, trans. Winthrip Wetherbee (rpt. N.Y. and London, 1973), pp. 107, 108.
page 55   "Lewis says . . ." *Letters*, p. 283.
page 67   "He said . . ." *Letters*, p. 207.
page 71   "Lewis said . . ." Unpublished letter to Miss Jacob, August 13, 1941.
page 72   "This Life-Force . . ." *Mere Christianity*, p. 35.
          "Lewis says . . ." "The Funeral of a Great Myth," *Christian Reflections*, p. 82ff.
page 73   "Lewis said he . . ." Unpublished letter to Arthur Clarke, December 7, 1945.
          "I look . . ." "Cross Examination," *God in the Dock* (Grand Rapids: Eerdmans, 1970), p. 267.
          "He was certain . . ." See "The Seeing Eye," *Christian Reflections* and "Religion and Rocketry," *The World's Last Night*.
          "No moonlit . . ." "The Seeing Eye," *Christian Reflections*, p. 172.
          "But if . . ." "Cross Examination," *God in the Dock*, p. 267.

"Lewis himself . . ." Unpublished letter to Mr. Kinter, July 30, 1954.

"Lewis claims . . ." Preface to *That Hideous Strength*.

page 74   "But Lewis . . ." Unpublished letter to Ms. Canfield, February 28, 1955.

page 75   "Lewis considered . . ." *Ibid*.

page 77   "When it . . ." W. H. Lewis, *C. S. Lewis: A Biography* (unpublished), February 28, 1956, p. 404.

"However, Lewis . . ." Unpublished letter to Mr. Evans, September 26, 1945.

page 79   "Lewis believed . . ." "Vivisection," *God in the Dock*, p. 224ff.

"Lewis believes that such . . ." See "The Humanitarian Theory of Punishment," and "On Punishment: A Reply to Criticism" in *God in the Dock*, pp. 287-294, 295-300.

page 80   "Though I . . ." *Surprised by Joy*, p. 137.

"He defined . . ." "On Obstinacy in Belief," *They Asked For a Paper* (London: Bles, 1962), p. 184.

page 81   "The boy . . ." "On Three Ways of Writing for Children," *Of Other Worlds*, pp. 29, 30.

page 83   "There are thus . . ." See "Meditation in a Toolshed," *God in the Dock*, pp. 212ff.

page 85   "The greatest . . ." G. K. Chesterton, *Orthodoxy* (1908; rpt. N.Y.: Image Books, 1959), p. 64.

"In *Miracles* . . ." *Miracles*, p. 167.

page 86   "At the outset . . ." "Preface" to D. E. Harding, *Hierarchy of Heaven and Earth* (London: Faber and Faber, 1952), p. 9.

page 87   "The naturalist . . ." *Miracles*, p. 10.

"The masters . . ." *Hierarchy of Heaven and Earth*, pp. 9, 10.

"As thinkers . . ." "Myth Became Fact," *God in the Dock*, p. 65.

page 88   "This is because . . ." "On Stories," *Of Other Worlds*, p. 18.

"In the enjoyment . . ." "Myth Became Fact," *God in the Dock*, p. 66.

page 89   "Instead, myth . . ." "Introduction" to George MacDonald, *Phantastes and Lilith* (1946; rpt. Grand Rapids: Eerdmans, 1964), pp. 10, 11.

page 91   "But Lewis . . ." "A Reply to Professor Haldane," *Of Other Worlds*, p. 78.

"Lewis says . . ." Unpublished notes to Fr. Milward, April 7, 1955.

page 93   "But Lewis . . ." Unpublished letters to W. L. Kinter, November 27, 1951 and March 28, 1953.

page 94   "Lewis says . . ." Unpublished letter, April 29, 1943.

page 96   "at last . . ." *Preface to Paradise Lost* (1942; rpt. London: OUP, 1977), p. 116. Though this quotation refers to Milton's idea of what an encounter with the unfallen Adam would be like, it seems entirely appropriate to apply it to Ransom's encounter with the King of Perelandria.

"Lewis admitted . . ." Unpublished letter to Jenkins, January 22, 1939.

"But Lewis says . . ." *Preface to Paradise Lost,* p. 100.
"Thus, Lewis . . ." *Letters,* p. 195.
"There are . . ." "The Weight of Glory," *The Weight of Glory* (1949; rpt. Grand Rapids: Eerdmans, 1975), p. 15.

page 97 "There is . . ." *They Asked For a Paper,* Chap. 9.
"Screwtape even . . ." *The Screwtape Letters* (N.Y.: Macmillan, 1961), p. 64.

page 100 "Lewis says . . ." *The Problem of Pain,* p. 98.
"One metaphor . . ." *Ibid.,* p. 42.

page 102 "In *Of* . . ." "A Reply to Professor Haldane," *Of Other Worlds,* p. 79.

page 107 "Lewis admitted . . ." Unpublished letter to Sr. Penelope, August 9, 1939.
"Although he . . ." Unpublished letter to Milton Society of America, December 1954.
"You have . . ." Unpublished letter to Miss Jacob, July 3, 1941.

page 109 "Lewis said . . ." *Ibid.* and unpublished letter to Sr. Penelope, August 9, 1939.

page 111 "There is . . ." "Christianity and Culture," *Christian Reflections,* p. 33.
"Evil, says Lewis . . ." W. H. Lewis, *C. S. Lewis: A Biography* (unpublished), January 11, 1954, p. 382.

page 113 "Part of . . ." *Ibid.*

page 114 "In *Preface* . . ." *Preface to Paradise Lost,* p. 100.

page 118 "Lewis warns . . ." Unpublished letter to Arthur Greeves, April 4, 1919.
"After all . . ." *The Great Divorce,* p. 69.
"For example . . ." "The Shoddy Lands," *Of Other Worlds,* p. 106.

page 119 "We often . . ." *Letters to Malcolm* (N.Y.: Harcourt, Brace, Jovanovich, 1963, 1964), p. 26.
"Lewis explains . . ." *The Four Loves* (N.Y.: Harcourt, Brace, Jovanovich, 1960), p. 28ff.

page 120 "Screwtape warns . . ." *The Screwtape Letters,* p. 60.
"Pleasures of . . ." *The Four Loves,* p. 32.

page 123 "Lewis writes . . ." "The Weight of Glory," *The Weight of Glory,* pp. 12, 13.

page 124 "It is . . ." *Surprised By Joy,* p. 16.
"In 'The . . ." *The Weight of Glory,* pp. 4, 5.

page 125 "This special . . ." "On Three Ways of Writing for Children," *Of Other Worlds,* p. 30.

page 141 "In a letter . . ." *Letters,* p. 284.
"Lewis also . . ." *Letters,* p. 280 and W. H. Lewis, *C. S. Lewis: A Biography* (unpublished), July 11, 1963, p. 465.

page 142 "Lewis noted . . ." Unpublished letter to Sr. Penelope, August 24, 1939.

page 146 **(Atlantean Circle)** *Letters,* p. 244.
(Avalon) *Letters,* p. 205.

page 148 **(Belbury)** A. F. Reddy, "The Else Unspeakable: An Introduction to the Fiction of C. S. Lewis" (Ph.D.: U. of Massachusetts, May 1972).

(Bent One) Unpublished letter to Miss Jacob, July 3, 1941.

page 149 **(Bragdon)** Unpublished letter to Vera Matthews Gebbert, October 31, 1949.

(Bultitude) Unpublished letter to W. H. Lewis, June 14, 1932; *Letters*, p. 244; W. H. Lewis, *C. S. Lewis: A Biography* (unpublished), February 10, 1952, p. 360.

page 153 **(Dimble)** Unpublished notes to Fr. Milward, April 7, 1955.

page 154 **(eldil)** *Letters*, p. 283; unpublished letter to Martin, July 10, 1957.

page 155 **(Filostrato)** Unpublished letter to Ms. Canfield, February 28, 1955.

page 156 **(Frost)** "A Reply to Professor Haldane," *Of Other Worlds*, p. 83.

page 157 **(Glundandra)** *Letters*, p. 284.

(green) Unpublished letter to Sr. Penelope, August 22, 1942.

(Green Lady) *Letters*, p. 195.

page 159 **(Head)** Hooper and Green, *C. S. Lewis: A Biography*, p. 174.

(Hingest) Unpublished letter to Ms. Canfield, February 28, 1955.

page 160 **(hnau)** *Letters*, p. 284.

(hross) Unpublished letter to Sr. Penelope, August 24, 1939.

page 161 **(Inner Ring)** "A Reply to Professor Haldane," *Of Other Worlds*, p. 79.

(Jules) Unpublished letter to Ms. Canfield, February 28, 1955.

page 163 **(MacPhee)** Unpublished notes to Fr. Milward, April 7, 1955.

page 164 **(Maleldil the Young)** Unpublished letter to Sr. Penelope, August 9, 1939; *Letters*, p. 284.

page 165 **(Merlin)** *Letters*, p. 207.

page 166 **(mice)** Unpublished letter to Hila N. Feil, June 3, 1953.

page 168 **(Northumberland)** W. H. Lewis, *C. S. Lewis: A Biography* (unpublished), March 27, 1963, p. 463.

(Numinor) *Letters*, p. 244; Humphrey Carpenter, *The Inklings* (Boston: Houghton Mifflin, 1979), p. 198.

page 170 **(pfifltrigg)** W. H. Lewis, *C. S. Lewis: A Biography* (unpublished), letter to Dr. Morgan, December 1949.

page 171 **(philologist)** Unpublished notes to Fr. Milward, April 7, 1955.

page 172 **(Ransom)** *Ibid.;* unpublished letter to W. L. Kinter, November 27, 1951 and March 28, 1953.

page 174 **(Seven Bears)** W. H. Lewis, *C. S. Lewis: A Biography* (unpublished), February 10, 1952; *Letters*, p. 244; unpublished letter to W. H. Lewis, June 14, 1932.

page 175 **(St. Anne's)** Unpublished letter to Mr. Kinter, July 30, 1954.

page 177 **(Third One)** Unpublished letter to Miss Jacob, July 3, 1941.

page 178 **(Thulcandra)** Hooper and Green, *C. S. Lewis: A biography*, p. 172.

(Tor) Carpenter, *The Inklings*, p. 182.

(Venus) *Arthurian Torso* (1948; rpt. Grand Rapids: Eerdmans,

1974), p. 287.
(Viritrilbia) *Letters*, p. 284.
page 179   **(Weston)** *Letters*, p. 167.